'This absolutely fascinating book takes the lens of mind various strands of professional behaviour and practice research to underpin her arguments in a way that is ligm. .. .. confidence that we should all be taking care of ourselves, our colleagues, and our pupils, not in some wishy-washy, feel-good way but in an intentional way that preserves and enhances energy rather than depleting it. There are some excellent case studies bringing this to life; we all need to hear from heads who don't work late or at weekends and who also lead stunningly successful schools. Highly recommended.'

**Mary Myatt**
*Education Writer and Curator of Myatt & Co*

'Stimulating and thought-provoking . . . a genuinely scholarly attempt to bring together very divergent views into something that doesn't fall apart when you shake it.'

**Ben Newmark**
*Deputy Head Teacher*

'Practical yet makes you reflect. A brilliantly helpful handbook for leaders and a timely reminder to slow down and take care of me, as this affects my ability to lead others.'

**Jane Manzone**
*Teacher, @HeyMissSmith*

'Aurora has a fresh, enlightening perspective and the book provides an insightful, original lens on some of the biggest challenges schools face.'

**Ed Vainker**
*CEO, Reach Foundation*

# Leading Mindfully for Healthy and Successful Schools

Schools are increasingly expected to improve mental health and well-being *and* academic outcomes for students. However, the debate about well-being and school improvement is often unhelpfully polarised with attachment-informed and restorative-justice approaches pitted against structures and systems that instil discipline. This book seeks to take a 'middle way', looking at how these perspectives might complement one another, and argues that healthy teacher-student relationships require an adult that is both attuned to their students' needs and able to hold boundaries with them.

Setting out a concept of leadership that is clear, compassionate and self-aware, *Leading Mindfully for Healthy and Successful Schools* draws on therapeutic and educational research to identify key strategies for improving well-being across schools that are sustainable in the long term. This book is divided into three sections – Leading Yourself, Leading School Culture and Leading in the Classroom – and the chapters cover the following:

- Interpersonal Neurobiology and the role that attachment plays in our work
- Self-care and how this can be built into school life
- The role of structures and relationships
- Building trust
- Radical inclusion
- Building calm and effective classrooms
- Healthy adult authority

With reflective activities, thought-provoking case studies and key takeaways for every chapter, this is an essential read for all current and aspiring school leaders.

**Aurora Reid** has worked as a senior leader in several schools. As a qualified DSL and SENDCo, she has led primarily on inclusion but has also held curriculum and teacher-development roles. She is passionate about inclusive leadership in the broadest sense, as that is how we build equity and care for all into the heart of our schools. Aurora is currently a consultant based in London. She blogs at streamlinedSENDCo.com.

# Leading Mindfully for Healthy and Successful Schools

## Beyond the Traditional Progressive Divide

Aurora Reid

Routledge
Taylor & Francis Group

LONDON AND NEW YORK

Cover image: © Getty Images

First published 2023
by Routledge
4 Park Square, Milton Park, Abingdon, Oxon OX14 4RN

and by Routledge
605 Third Avenue, New York, NY 10158

*Routledge is an imprint of the Taylor & Francis Group, an informa business*

*British Library Cataloguing-in-Publication Data*
A catalogue record for this book is available from the British Library

*Library of Congress Cataloging-in-Publication Data*
Names: Reid, Aurora, author.
Title: Leading mindfully for healthy and successful schools : beyond the traditional progressive divide / Aurora Reid.
Description: Abingdon, Oxon ; New York : Routledge, 2023. | Includes bibliographical references and index.
Identifiers: LCCN 2022003738 | ISBN 9781032056357 (hardback) | ISBN 9781032056364 (paperback) | ISBN 9781003198482 (ebook)
Subjects: LCSH: Educational leadership. | Mindfulness (Psychology) | Reflective teaching. | Teacher-student relationships.
Classification: LCC LB2806 .R373 2023 | DDC 371.2/011—dc23/eng/20220503
LC record available at https://lccn.loc.gov/2022003738

ISBN: 978-1-032-05635-7 (hbk)
ISBN: 978-1-032-05636-4 (pbk)
ISBN: 978-1-003-19848-2 (ebk)

DOI: 10.4324/9781003198482

Typeset in Melior
by Apex CoVantage, LLC

# Contents

## *Section Three: Leading in the Classroom*

# Acknowledgements

I have had the privilege of having so many guides in both my personal and professional life, individuals who are referenced or featured in this book. They have offered me an alternative vision of how we might lead more mindfully. Under this guidance, I have built a better relationship with myself and others and have become a better teacher and leader.

The seed of this book came from conversations with my yoga teacher (and auntie) Zoë, so my first thank-you goes to you for your hospitality and inspiration.

Clare and Chereece, thank you for your light and wisdom in darker times.

Conor, thanks for the timely feedback that forced me to confront and tell the real story.

Charlotte, thank you for bringing clarity, levity and truth.

Alison, for being the one who earthed me, thank you for the nourishment, encouragement and wisdom.

Mum and Phil, thank you for the unending support, the inspiration, the chats and the cheerleading – and for the introduction to Porges.

Thank you, DBNS for all your inspiration and input.

Chloe, thank you for being a glorious pacesetter and proofreader.

Thank you to Dad and the boys and to Bids in particular for a stroke of genius with the cover.

And thank you to my bois, burglars, greedies and fiddlers for being divine, supportive humans.

Thank you, Annamarie and Molly, for your hard work and pertinent questions.

Thank you to the reviewers and edu-tweeters, particularly to Clare for her gracious foreword.

Finally, thank you to the aunties, mentors and managers who have shaped me.

# Foreword

*Clare Sealy*

This is a book about creating school cultures where people can feel safe – staff as well as students. That shouldn't be a big ask, yet somehow it is. Many teachers do not feel safe. This is not right.

Something is not right within our profession when every Sunday night you can read tweets about teachers feeling sick with dread about the week ahead. Something's not right when the attrition rate of early-career teachers leaving the profession is so high. Something's not right when you read about the appalling ways in which some leaders treat their staff in truly toxic schools. What is this sickness within the teaching profession, and what can we do about it?

Many of us are drawn to teaching because of a deep-seated desire to make a difference, to do some good in the world. Many of us are driven by a sense of moral purpose that teaching has the potential to channel. Consider the mission statement of Teach First, 'Fighting to make our education system work for every child.' Teaching is cast as a noble and heroic endeavour within which we fight, battle and strive to rescue those we seek to teach from the foes of disadvantage, racism and powerlessness. With such formidable foes to combat, it is no wonder one's own needs are overlooked. It is no wonder the needs of colleagues are seen as trivial, an indulgent distraction from what really matters.

It's easy to dismiss such motivations as manifestations of a saviour complex: people motivated by a need to feel good about themselves which can only be fed when helping someone else – ideally someone weaker and needier – and which involves as a badge of honour sacrificing your own interests, well-being and sense of psychological safety in service of the noble cause. But I doubt for most of us it is as clear-cut as that; not all desire to help others is the manifestation of pathology. Most of us are probably a bewildering mix of motives, some of which are more problematic than others. But developing the self-knowledge to understand our motivations will allow us to teach and lead others in ways that are both healthy and successful.

This book argues that developing as a leader involves not only growing the knowledge of your craft but also your self-knowledge. If we don't do this and leave our unexamined motives to run riot, there are three possible outcomes. We run the risk of burning ourselves out, hence the high attrition rate, the Sunday dread, the feelings of utter exhaustion in the holidays. Or we might become more and more controlling of those we seek to lead, insisting they conform absolutely to the battle plan we have in our heads, in which we, the heroic leader, bravely take our troops into the fray. In the most toxic schools, staff are dispensable ideology fodder, fuel consumed to feed the grandiose dreams of selfless service by deluded leaders drunk on their own visions of heroism. Or we become furious with those we cast as objects of rescue in our heroic pantomime, particularly if they don't seem to want to cooperate in being rescued very much. Or all three could happen.

If you have even a little bit of saviour complex within you, being a teacher is not a safe place to be psychologically. You will feel under threat. Either you will feel that you are never good enough, or you will be anxious that your colleagues are not up to your high standards and therefore need constant hectoring from you, or you will be outraged by the children who let you down by failing to be sufficiently res-cuable. All of these are further compounded by external accountability pressures over which you have no control and whose narrative you simultaneously loathe yet seek approval from.

Against such a waste of what was originally an honourable impulse to make a difference, here we have a book that bids us calm down, slow down, breathe, reflect and learn about ourselves and our impact on others. It's a book about finding safety for yourself, creating places of safety for those you seek to lead and for the children you serve.

It's a book that refuses to seek the pseudo safety of the Twitter gang, where you are only afforded safety if you stick to the right side – be that 'trad' or 'prog' – 'liking' those on the approved list and denouncing those in the other camp. In this book, you will find Reid drawing from the wisdom of both Tom Bennett and Paul Dix, for example, not such an immiscible combination as some would have us think. The book eschews false binaries and embraces dyads such as warm strict-ness, knowledge and love, Cognitive Science and the science of psychological safety drawn from polyvagal theory. Once you feel secure in your own self, you don't need to hoard virtue as if it were a finite commodity we need to battle over. You can let others be virtuous too, even those you disagree with. Virtue is a renew-able resource after all.

The first part of the book is therefore focused on learning to lead yourself. This is the section of the book that the self-identified 'trad' reader might find less familiar and more challenging as it introduces us to Interpersonal Neurobiology, attach-ment theory and mindfulness, which, it is fair to say, are not traditionally 'trad' staples. Though presumably, you wouldn't have picked up a book called *Leading Mindfully* if you were implacably hostile to ranging beyond safe 'trad' territory! Letting go of the distorting influence of any saviour complex will require the set-ting aside of ego and attending to both the emotional and logical parts of both our work and ourselves.

The second section is about leading a school culture grounded in both structures and relationships, promoting both knowledge and love and accountability without fear, in a place of genuine safety for all. When teachers feel safe, they radiate safety to others and are therefore better placed to help dysregulated students or for staff to regain equilibrium.

After the book takes us on an inner journey away from ego and establishes a culture of safety for our school, for staff and students alike, the final section describes how we are then to use many of the tools already on offer, such as the classroom management strategies in Teach Like a Champion and use the fruits of Cognitive Science well to enable our students to become empowered through the sharing of powerful knowledge.

It's a welcome resource to help us create schools where staff, as well as students, can thrive.

# Introduction

## My Story

I knew something had to change when I found myself slumped in my own hallway, unable to move. It was 6.45 in the morning, on a school day. I had bent down to put my shoes on, and until the adrenaline of being 'late' kicked in, I found I simply could not get back up. This was emotional exhaustion manifesting itself in a profoundly physical way.

Months of literally running from classroom to duty to meetings with barely time to use the toilet – let alone eat – had taken its toll on my physical health.

Until this point, my tendency was to work harder when things were difficult. Outwardly I had thrived. However, I did not always have the emotional support I needed. Every time I stopped, like so many teachers, I got really sick. The parts of my life that were not work suffered. However, with rest, diet and yoga, I preserved just enough of my health to continue.

During this time, I had the opportunity to learn from some incredible leaders – many of whom are referenced in this book. Together we raised a school from special measures and transformed it into the most improved in London. These results did not come at the expense of relationships or a broad educational experience but in a truly sustainable way. Being part of a team where you could see the impact of your actions made the trade up feel worth it. We knew we were making a huge difference in one of the most vulnerable communities in the city.

However, when I found myself in a different environment, at a school that was not only struggling but also did not recognise or support my capacity to change it, no longer was my work celebrated. Instead I was punished for putting my head above the parapet. Yet at the same time, I found a staff and student body desperate for support. It was a heartbreaking bind, and I broke physically.

However, rather than recognising that there was something unwell in the environment, it was suggested that I was not cut out for the job. I did not know it at the time, but this turned out to be a gift. Though not for reasons implied, it was true: I was not cut out for a 60+ hour week. No one should be.

DOI: 10.4324/9781003198482-1

So instead of continuing to work in an ineffective and unhealthy way, I chose to walk away. I took time out to reassess, to be in nature, and grew vegetables for a while in the sun. In that space, this book was born.

In choosing to slow down, I have had to become comfortable with the truth of my own humanity. I have had courage – first and foremost with myself – and went against cultural norms that perceive asking for help as a lack of resilience. This process has not been something I could think or action plan myself into. It has come about through a softening and a loosening, by doing less and being less 'in my head'. Yoga and mindfulness have supported this.

This book is for people like me, those who work with people like me and those who might be more like me than they have yet realised. It reflects my own story of going too fast and ignoring my body. I have as much experience of what does not make a healthy and successful school as what does. And whilst I achieved many things that I am proud of, in my relatively short career, not all of them have been sustainable. This is, therefore, an attempt to gather what I have learnt and share it. In the words of John Tomsett,[1] 'This much I know'.

## This Much I Know

Toxic schools come in all shapes and sizes. There is no unifying ideology or approach. What they have in common is they fail their staff, their students or both. When as leaders, we are not connected to our own centre of health and humanity, when we work like crazy, we not only make ourselves sick, but we also leave no room to listen and respond to what our communities actually need. Our survival instincts, or attachment behaviours, kick in, stifling our capacity to think clearly or creatively.

It is easy to get into school shaming when cultures are unhealthy or leaders get it wrong, but schools are operating in intensely difficult conditions. What is more, we all come with our individual histories and complexities, even those at the top. We are living in a time that is sick, and much of what we do in schools accentuates this sickness.

However, if we chose to take positions of power, we have a duty, to the colleagues and young people that we lead, to check, challenge and support ourselves. This book will suggest that by doing this, we can help ourselves and our schools to thrive.

## The Challenge of Our Times

Our lifestyles are increasingly fast-paced. So are many of our schools. We are more connected than ever through technology and yet simultaneously disconnected from ourselves and each other. The evolutionary architecture of our brains is not wired to cope with the pressure and pace of this modern world. There is a mental health crisis in young people and adults alike, and this pressure is one of the many contributing factors.

The expectation that schools can 'fix' these problems is immense. They are expected to do more and more to support young people's well-being, alongside educating them, with ever-shrinking resources. Yet schools are also subject to the same stresses and pressures that have led to the crisis in the first place.

As a result, some schools have become frantically busy places. Despite the policies, action plans and interventions, the problems persist. High teacher burnout and poor retention rates are symptomatic of this. Desperate to find a silver bullet, we have become locked in binary debates. Whether they are about knowledge or skills, discipline or relationships, phonics or reading for meaning, we swing between *traditional* or *progressive* approaches and initiative after initiative without enough time to breathe or reflect.

At the root of these debates is a dualism in Western thinking that casts reason against emotion, the head against the heart and the sensible against the idealistic. Traditional (trad) approaches are typically viewed as teacher centred, valuing strict discipline and the passing on of knowledge. Critiqued as being a throwback to Gradgrindian Victorian classrooms, this approach is, somewhat unfairly, associated with conservative politics. Progressive (prog) education is associated with the left wing and is characteristically student centred, with an emphasis on relationships and the development of skills. The charge levied at it, also unfairly in my view, is that it is naive and unrigorous, meaning that it ultimately fails the very young people it sets out to support.

This discourse is particularly polarised right now, with 'culture wars' stoked on social media. It can seem easier, especially when we feel under threat, to retreat into one's echo chamber or a hold firm in a binary position. We either dig our heels in – working harder, not smarter – or oscillate between binary positions, starting initiative after initiative and exhausting ourselves in the process.

However, this book will argue that if we slow down, we will see that much of the truth, of what really makes a healthy and successful school, is found in the middle ground. A mindful approach can help us traverse these tired debates by giving us space to pause and just be with things as they are.

## What Does It Mean to Be Mindful?

Mindfulness is a secularised and Westernised form of Buddhism that is very much en vogue right now. An increasing number of studies are finding it to have profoundly positive effects on the physical and mental health of both individuals and organisational cultures, so much so that Oxford University have dedicated an entire research centre to the topic.[2]

Jon Kabat-Zinn, hailed by many as bringing mindfulness to the West, frames it as 'the awareness that emerges through paying attention on purpose, in the present moment, and nonjudgmentally to the unfolding of experience, moment by moment' (Kabat-Zinn, 2003, p. 145).

Stopping to notice without evaluating or needing to put things in a box runs counter to how we work in schools. Success is so often measured through high-stakes grading, and there is always more to do and understand. However, this is precisely why a mindful approach to leadership is so valuable. Creating space to pay attention, non-judgmentally, to what is going on in ourselves and in our schools is key to real change.

## Embracing Paradox

When we stop and look at things as they are, we see there are no clear-cut answers. The challenges that we face in school – learning, mental health and social justice – are complex and interconnected problems. They cannot just be 'fixed'.

However, there is truth and possibility to be found within the messiness and the nuance. Whilst we cannot fix it, we can make a difference. Polarised thinking neither reflects what works, nor does it recognise the hopeful fact that almost everyone working in education wants the same thing – that is, what is best for the children. Good ideas can come from both sides (and between) the divide. We do not need to be restricted.

To lead a healthy and successful school is to inhabit the space of paradox. This opens up rather than closes down possibilities. We find that strong systems are integral to building good relationships that we do not have to prioritise outcomes at the expense of the whole child and that to be able to offer more to others, we must start with ourselves.

By slowing down and making time for our own needs, we are able to think more clearly and create more space within our institutions. This enables those we lead to do the same for the students and families we serve.

When we feel safe and secure in ourselves, we can focus on what really matters. The book will explore how mindful leaders refuse to hide behind a fear of Ofsted or any other external evaluation. Instead, they calmly and courageously scrap outdated or unnecessary processes and, in doing so, create warm, safe and focused environments where everyone can learn. Knowing that the needs of their students cannot be met at the expense of their staff, it considers how leaders might do the work, of self-reflection and self-care, so they can show up in the best possible way for their communities, what I will call *leading mindfully*.

## Wise Leaders

This different form of leadership is already underway in pockets of schools. There are wise leaders who are showing us the way, finding common ground between those voices that might seem more traditional and those that are more progressive. I have had the privilege of working with and learning from the colleagues whose stories come through, in case studies, across the book.

We will see how they are embracing paradox and nuance and leading their schools with both love and knowledge[3] – that is choosing to go beyond a binary that pits building relationships against implementing systems that enable consistency, teacher authority against students' needs or developing skills against learning facts.

There is also a groundswell beyond education, as a multitude of disciplines and wisdom traditions coalesce with a remarkably similar message, that the keys to health and well-being are balance and integration. They are demonstrating how, through knowledge of and respect for the embodied and relational nature of the mind, there are possibilities for real change and for a literal rewiring of our brains.

This book will draw on the emerging discipline of Interpersonal Neurobiology, to argue that we do not need to be bound by the confines of 'trad' or 'prog' nor be restricted to either objective or subjective forms of knowing. We can draw what works from both sides of the debate. It is possible to be guided by the evidence *and* have a heartfelt response to our own community's needs. Furthermore, it is not clear-cut. Traditional methods can support progressive aims, whilst some progressive methods can in fact do the opposite. For example, there is liberatory potential in passing on powerful knowledge,[4] and if we are too student-centred in the classroom, we run the risk of neglecting our teachers, which is no good for anyone.

## This Book

The book is in three sections that build on one another: Leading Yourself, Leading School Culture and Leading in the Classroom. The first section draws on the research from Interpersonal Neurobiology and the tradition of mindfulness to make the case that knowing and taking care of yourself are the first steps to creating a healthy and successful school. Section Two explores how these principles can be applied to building school culture and the strategic decisions that are both a result and cause of a more mindful approach. Finally, Section Three examines how this can be implemented into the classroom.

This book is geared towards those with the institutional power to make strategic change. However, those who do not currently have formal leadership roles also have a role to play in changing school culture from the ground up. I firmly believe that if you lead a class of students, you are a leader. What is more, the final section is specifically focused on classroom practice. This is because as leaders, it is important to consider how our ideas will actually be implemented in individual classrooms. It guards against them simply being 'lofty ideals'.

This book is designed with a busy leader in mind. Every chapter begins with an outline of what the chapter will cover and ends with a short summary. There are several practical activities and case studies which offer a toolkit that teachers, leaders and aspiring leaders can use to support themselves to be healthy and successful in their work.

## What the Book Is Not

It is perhaps important to add that this book is not about meditation. Whilst it does contain some tools for building mindful reflection into your life, it explores the principles and science behind why cultivating an attitude of presence and awareness, or mindfulness, can allow us to be more effective in our leadership, both in terms of our relationships and getting results.

That is not to imply that it is a fully finished project. The book is deliberately titled *Leading Mindfully* and not *Mindful Leadership*. Mindfulness is a process, not a state to achieve. It is, therefore, an invitation into a conversation about how we might lead schools more calmly, thoughtfully and reflectively.

Though you will find practical tools to bring this to life, they are not a blueprint to follow. The intention is that you will use the principles and tools to find your own way, in your own context. Leadership is not always neat, tidy or comfortable. To address the challenges of our job, we first must meet them in their complexity.

Furthermore, whilst many of the leaders featured in the book echo my sentiment – that we need to set our ego aside and think and communicate clearly if we are going to build healthy and successful schools – they also bring to life the decisions that they make and the challenges they face, making this happen in their day-to-day practice.

With this, I offer a note of caution: we cannot just take what others do wholesale and expect it to work in our own contexts. The summaries and resources should not be used alone or seen as a 'silver bullet'. Much of what these leaders do best is difficult to capture on a page. Their actions not only need to be understood but also lived and breathed. The book repeatedly extols how important it is to slow down our thinking and build long-term sustainable shifts rather than simply 'ticking a box'. Thus, I invite you to pause, breathe and enjoy reading the book slowly and mindfully.

## Notes

1 Read the blog series entitled *This much I know* at johntomsett.com.
2 More information at oxfordmindfulness.org.
3 This is a notion introduced by the head teacher Carly Waterman that will be expounded in Section Two.
4 This is a term coined by Michael Young that refers to the power of knowledge to enable us to go beyond our experiences. Young (2014, p. 74) describes that knowledge is powerful 'if it predicts, if it explains, if it enables you to envisage alternatives'.

# SECTION ONE
# Leading Yourself

# Leading Mindfully

This chapter will do the following:

- Make the case for a more mindful form of leadership
- Set out three principles of leading mindfully
- Suggest where we might begin to bring this into our practice

## The Cost of Our Work

Schools can be frantically busy places and stressful for everyone involved. These are not have the optimum conditions for a healthy and successful education. As leaders we care deeply about this. Yet in trying to make things better, we seem to have lost our way. In her foreword to Mary Myatt's (2020) book *Back on Track: Fewer Things, Greater Depth*, Clare Sealy sums it up brilliantly.

> It's not even a case of not being able to see the wood for the trees – some schools are so wedded to ticking off items in their i-Spy Book of Educational Improvement that they have forgotten the point of the whole endeavour.
>
> (2020)

New and competing agendas bring stress and the threat of burnout to the already complex art of teaching. According to NFER data, from 2016 to 2017, 9.9% of teachers left the workforce compared to 9.2% from 2010 to 2011 (Worth, 2018). For secondary schools alone, the figures are even higher, with 10.4% of secondary teachers leaving the workforce from 2016 to 2017. This has become an area of national concern. In (2019b) OFSTED undertook a survey of teachers' well-being across 2,000 schools. In response, teachers cited excessive working hours, more time spent out of the classroom attending to marking and administration, and endless meetings as significantly affecting their job satisfaction. An OECD survey (2019) conducted in 48 countries found that teachers and school leaders in the UK are working longer days than in any other country apart from Japan.

DOI: 10.4324/9781003198482-3

Our system and many of our schools are injurious to our health. Howard points to a 2016 study that indicated that 73% of teachers said their workload was having a serious impact on their physical health (2020, p. 40). What we have come to see as the inevitable end of term illness is actually a known psychological phenomenon called 'leisure sickness' (*ibid.*). Furthermore, Tom Bennett cites a range of figures from a 2018 survey that found that 11% of teachers have been physically assaulted, one in seven threatened and more than half verbally abused by pupils (Bennett, 2020).

## The Cost of Leadership

There is particular strain placed on leaders. Beyond the long hours required, there is an emotional cost linked to 'being the boss' all the time. The effort involved in presenting a particular emotional stance as part of one's work role is defined as 'emotional labour'. In her landmark study of flight attendants, Hochschild (1983) documented the toxic stress that resulted from the requirement on them to act a certain way as part of their employment. These findings are applicable for school leaders too. Left unchecked, the dissonance between your own feelings and how you must present can cause all sorts of problems. Suppressing your own needs and physical responses in the name of the greater good or consistency or just to maintain a professional persona in challenging circumstances, can take a significant toll on your physical and mental well-being. This is often amplified as we move into leadership.

If we are honest with ourselves, how many of us feel secure in our schools? How able are we to be ourselves? There is so much pressure on us from above and below, it can feel hard to do so. I know that for many years, through a combination of external pressure and my own baggage, I did not feel at home in myself, in my body, in my school. Palpitations, sweating and a dry mouth were my daily experience, and fatigue, muscle pain and illness the accompaniment to my weekends and holidays. Not only was this an unpleasant experience, but being wound up that tightly meant I did not do my best work.

The already difficult context that schools operate in has been exacerbated by the isolation, fear, economic impacts, shifting goal posts and endless marking that the pandemic has brought. Recent research by the Anna Freud Centre indicates that many young people, already struggling pre-lockdown at what is described as the 'sub-clinical range', have moved up into the clinical range (Fonagy, 2021). Our staff are suffering too, with recent Teacher Tapp data indicating that anxiety rates are high amongst staff with Head Teachers consistently reporting the highest levels of anxiety (2021).

## Survival Mode

As school leaders, we can often feel too busy being reactive to stop and do the strategic work.

As a special educational needs coordinator (SENDCo), I knew that the thing that would make the biggest difference to the life chances of young people with SEND was improving the quality of the teaching they received. However, I was too often caught up battling for high-needs-provision, timetabling or just fighting fires when a dysregulated student invariably got removed from a lesson and needed an adult to calm them down.

As a safeguarding lead, I knew the key to ensuring young people were safe was to make their school experience constant and predictable and ensuring there were good systems in place for effective joined-up working. However, so much of my day was spent reacting to urgent safeguarding alerts and disclosures that I would rarely have the time, energy or brain capacity to do the big-picture work.

The quality of our interactions also suffers when we are exhausted. If pushed for time, we do not always give our colleagues or students the attention or the empathetic responses they need. Our brains, and therefore our practice, go into survival mode (the neuroscience of which will be explored further in Chapter 2).

This can change, but the paradox is that we get there by doing less. There is a Zen proverb that says, 'You should sit in meditation for twenty minutes every day – unless you're too busy; then you should sit for an hour.' Whilst I have promised this is not a book about meditation, the sentiment stands: taking time to breathe and zoom out pays dividends.

## An Invitation to Do Things Differently

It does not have to be this way. As we move into a post-Covid-19 world, there is more to do than ever before to 'catch up' and get back to some form of normality. Yet in creating this 'new normal', there is an opportunity, an invitation to do things differently, more mindfully. The pandemic has shone a sharp light on how fragile and interconnected we all are. It has forced us to confront what really matters: health, kindness, community. It has revealed the necessity of teachers standing in front of students, sharing their knowledge of their subjects *and* drawing on their knowledge of their students. None of this can be supplemented by screens; you cannot just 'google it'. The value of the human connection with teachers and students is priceless, particularly for those who are most vulnerable.

There is a lot to do to make our schools safe havens in which learning flourishes. We need to get *back on track* and remember, as Sealy says, 'the point of the whole endeavour'. Yet our initiatives to address this often make things worse. In reaction, we slip into our default mode of doing more – another audit or checklist, a mandatory well-being event – to try and fix the problem. A culture of overwork, quick fixes and putting our humanity aside quickly sours good intentions. Furthermore, when we are stressed, at least over time, we do not see as clearly as we might, nor are we able to relate as well to others.

This is where a mindful approach to leadership comes into play. We need to find a way to support everyone's well-being that is sustainable and gets the job done.

And it starts with us. If we are burnt out or our decision-making is led by fear, this comes at the detriment of those we lead and serve. It is our challenge as leaders, amongst the pressure, to carve out the space to stop, to look at things as they really are in all their messy complexity.

We cannot do this by following the same old patterns that leave us exhausted and scared. Curiosity, clear-headedness and space are required for learning to happen. As Myatt says, 'The likelihood is we will not be prepared to enter this space [of deep learning] if we are concerned about our image, how we come across, about what other people think of us. We have to put those factors to one side and accept that the pursuit of clarity requires us to let go of some of our preconception' (Myatt, 2020, p. 352).

## Courageous Leadership

If we can find a way to let go of notions of perfection and the fear of what others think of us, accepting instead that we are always learning, we are able to more truthfully appraise how things *are*. Then we can begin to ask the questions that lead to *real* change. For example, the less concerned we are with our own performance in the classroom, the more able we are to listen and take on board others' feedback. Or we could approach that scary audit that must be completed each year as a tool to genuinely support us to know how to improve. If this audit could be something more than a task to be ticked off to prove our compliance, not only would we feel less stressed, but there would be more space to move the schools we lead forward.

This acceptance requires the recognition of our humanness, that progress is not linear and that we all need time and space to embed new learning as well as intelligent systems that serve people, not processes. Thus, at regular intervals, mindful leaders pause and reflect. From here they can clearly see what the priorities should be and what can be streamlined. Then they make space for others to do the same (Figure 1.1).

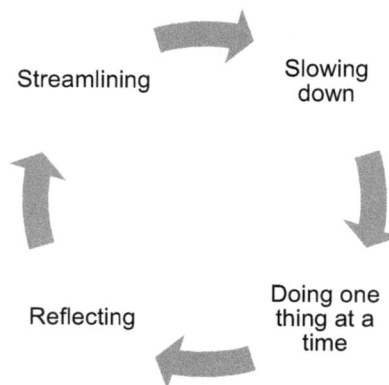

Streamlining — Slowing down — Doing one thing at a time — Reflecting

**Figure 1.1** Graphic that explains the principles and process of leading mindfully, that is first slowing down, committing to one thing at a time, reflecting on the process and then working out where things can be streamlined or refined further

# Finding Clarity

Getting clear on where to spend one's limited time and energy is both a cause and effect of mindfulness. Drawing on the work of Mary Myatt (2016, 2020) and Jamie Thom (2018), as well as a number of clear-headed leaders whom I have had the honour of working with, I will discuss the role that streamlining and minimalism can play in the wider school culture and in our classrooms in Sections Two and Three.

Once we strip things back, we can see what drains us, and it is usually lack of purpose and connection. What clears and energises us is feeling supported and like you are achieving something.

Letting go of the myth of multitasking is also key. In doing this, you are able to be present in what you are doing that moment. Surprisingly, for some of us who believe we were being efficient by doing a lot of things at once, rejecting multitasking can transform your concentration and your relationships.

As with the structure of this book, you must start with your own practice. To begin with, we must be the change we want to see, bringing calm and purpose and providing opportunities for reflection. We must shield our schools from the things that do not matter and which can distort practice – endless bureaucracy and unhelpful fear generated through high-stakes accountability.

Let's start with how we use our time, organise our space and speak to ourselves. Then this way of working can be extended to our whole school priorities, the teams we manage, our classroom and the way that our schools relate to their communities. Mindful leadership is a democratising and iterative practice. As it builds over time, it creates more space and brings more people in. But it starts at the top with us.

# Three Principles

There are three key principles that broadly underpin a mindful approach to leadership. These are meeting your own emotional needs first, going beyond binary thinking and leading without ego. If they sound a little abstract, please persevere. They are rooted in both science and the experience of wise and successful leaders.

## i) Begin With Your Own Emotional Needs

The notion of leading yourself is the first principle of leading mindfully. The Buddhist tradition has long understood what science is now empirically proving; we are interconnected. Therefore, the well-being of young people and the well-being of the adults supporting them are integrated. As Sergiovanni states, 'Teachers are best able to serve students when they themselves are adequately served' (2005, p. 101). When we are healthy in mind and body, we are better placed to enrich others. And crucially, when our work is successful, it is enriching for us as well as those we lead.

For some of us who are so burnt out, the notion that we could love our work, feel we have purpose yet not be exhausted at the end of the day might seem alien. However, it is possible. As Parker J. Palmer puts it, 'In a culture that sometimes equates work with suffering, it is revolutionary to suggest that the best inward sign of vocation is deep gladness – revolutionary but true' (Palmer, 2017, p. 31). Finding joy in our work will benefit us and our students. Yet it is not easy to do if we are caught in the endless hamster wheel that schools too often can be.

For many the notion of 'self-care' conjures up images of spa days, and it is perhaps hard to see its immediate impact on the day-to-day reality of our schools. However, slowing down and taking time for oneself has a strong grounding in science.

Interpersonal Neurobiology is a multidisciplinary field that draws on neuroscience, biology, psychology and psychotherapy as well as wisdom traditions from around the world, including Buddhism. This emerging discipline is illuminating the ways in which the embodied brain and our relationships interact to shape our mental lives (Siegal, 2012). Studies have shown (Porges, 2017; Siegal, 2012) that our emotional and physiological state has a direct impact on those around us. Through our affective signals – our body language, facial expressions, tone of voice – we physically regulate (or dysregulate) the psychological and physiological state of those around us (Porges, 2017). This process has roots in an infant's absolute dependence on its caregiver. We have evolved to be deeply and biologically interconnected to those around us (Siegal, 2012). Mirror neurons fire when an animal acts and when it observes the same action performed by another (Rizzolatti & Craighero, 2004). Transposed into the school environment, this wiring means that, if we come to the classroom or a staff meeting in a calm state, we physically create a sense of felt security in others; if we are dysregulated, then others feel that too.

## ii) Beyond Binary Thinking

In a post-Trump (hopefully) and post-Brexit social-media-fuelled world, complex issues are too often set up as binary choices. The discourse quickly becomes polarised on both sides. Education is no exception, dividing along tired 'trad' or 'prog' lines. The reality is of course far messier and more complex. For example, structures are key to autonomy and boundaries are essential for healthy relationships. Furthermore, you can have the most thorough, evidence-based system, but if it is not implemented with love, if people do not feel valued, then it is doomed to fail. Crucially though, our values are brought to life in a framework of skills and knowledge that enable us to follow through on our lofty intentions (Waterman, 2020). If we are going to be successful in the long term, then we have to engage with these paradoxes. This is the second principle of leading mindfully.

These false dichotomies have roots in a much deeper intellectual split between reason and emotion that suggests that relationships and feelings do not influence cognition. This could not be further from the truth. Neville illustrates how emotions play a significant part in learning and brain development, shaping 'both what students see and hear and the ways they process it' (Neville, 2013). Our felt sense of security has very real consequences for our capacity to think clearly and creatively. At a most basic level, if we are hypervigilant, our energy is diverted as we scan for threat instead of being present. As such, our working memory will not have space to process the task in·hand. Furthermore, severe stress can inhibit the formation of new memories, leading to a less developed schema (mental models of information). This in turn, places more stress on the working memory as new information cannot so easily be assimilated into existing frameworks.

This is also why *knowing* what to do is not always enough. When it comes to making change, whether in our personal or professional lives, we also must be in the right space emotionally and in our bodies to be able to see it through. We must have what is referred to as a 'felt sense of security'. Knowing this fact can help us understand why, despite being given a clear rationale for change, some colleagues or students may stick doggedly to old ways. It also reminds us to attend to culture and our own sense of felt security. Some leaders seem to have an ineffable ability to absorb stress, remain in their integrity and make clear-headed decisions even in adversity. I suggest that this is not actually ineffable at all, but neither is it entirely a result of rational thinking. When we start to consider the role of the body and the sense of safety in the workings of the mind, this can be illuminated.

As yet, these conversations have not worked themselves into the mainstream educational discourse. In recent years there has been an explosion in educators' understanding of Cognitive Science, which has had a direct impact on curriculum planning and classroom practice. I believe we need a similar revolution in terms of understanding the role of emotions, relationships and felt security in learning. If, as an educational, community we can harness knowledge of how the brain and body functions, what happens to it under stress and how it can be modified (what is referred to as neuroplasticity), we can use this knowledge to improve both learning and relationships. If we are to take the definition of Kirschner, Sweller, and Clark (2006, p. 75) that is popular with cognitive scientists that 'learning is a change in long-term memory', then we must also attend to the role of feelings, particularly feeling safe, in the learning process. Taking time to rest and reflect is good for you, your students and the teams you lead, and not just in terms of their well-being; it will actually help them learn more.

The discipline of Interpersonal Neurobiology helps us by explaining why we can know something cognitively yet have this reasoning become compromised when we are under stress. That is how, despite best intentions, we often fall back into old patterns, as well as the ways in which we physically pass on stress to those surrounding us. This next chapter aims to explore learnings from attachment theory and polyvagal theory to explain not only how we function under stress but also how we can rewire and reconfigure our responses. The chapter seeks to make explicit what some mindful leaders do implicitly, not just in their schools but also to themselves, and how this allows them to communicate more clearly and become more 'in the now' or more *mindful*. In doing so, the chapter provides a roadmap for teacher leaders to not only support their own well-being but also be more flexible and creative in response to others.

## iii) Leading Without Ego

Mindful leaders can set their ego aside and be the adult in the room. This is the third principle of *leading mindfully*.

What I mean by ego in the context of this book is the protective and self-serving part of ourselves that particularly emerges when we are under stress. Where there is fear generated by external pressure, the ego fires up. It is much easier to be liked (be that by staff, students or Ofsted), but mindful leaders do what is in the best interests of their schools even when that means being temporarily unpopular.

Stepping away from a place of certainty can be scary. It often feels simpler and safer to resort to binary positions. Tragically, it can sometimes even feel like a choice between getting the job done and one's values. However, doing so is dangerous. When we move away from a focus on the children and their learning towards performance for an external audience, whether that be Ofsted, Ofqual, league tables or social media, we do damage – not only to those young people that we are there to serve but also to ourselves. This is because our sense of meaning as teachers is deeply connected to our authenticity. If we try and 'game' the system, evidencing progress at the expense of real learning, it sucks the purpose out of our difficult and emotionally challenging job.

A mindful approach seeks to reorient us away from performance and towards the things that really matter. In this way, as Mary Myatt says, our values are 'lived, not laminated' (2007). That means we walk the walk day in and day out (even when it is unfashionable or exhausting) not for approval or for Ofsted or Twitter or because we fear reprisals from parents but because it is the right thing to do.

Doing so is not easy. Implementing and maintaining a culture that ensures that school is a secure base for all can be testing. Children (and adults) will not always like the rules nor see the immediate benefit of them. To consistently be the adult like this can be a challenge, to do so under stress even more so. We must have big arms and broad shoulders, much like a parent.

In fact, Popper and Mayseless's research (2003) demonstrates that leadership has many similarities to good parenting. They both require loving attunement to another's needs *and* clearly held boundaries, not one or the other. Again we come to another paradox. The corollary of this fact about leadership and parenting is that understanding parenting and attachment styles can help us in our work. The attachment-aware leader can recognise the defences that the ego puts up and hold them safely. By doing this, everyone – including themselves – can stay aligned with their purpose.

Secure leaders do achieve this without being reflective. They have their ear to the ground and are prepared to change if things are not working. Doing so requires the strength to trust, to be okay with not controlling or knowing everything, the strength to hold others to account and the discernment to know which is needed.

To have these qualities is not always easy. The nature of being this kind of leader means you are vulnerable. What is more, we all carry the baggage of being human, including our own experiences of being parented. Whilst we might never avoid our egos altogether – and it is not the intention of this book to suggest that we should – self-awareness matters. Without it, in these vulnerable and stressful situations, we can inadvertently end up triggering others' trauma as well as our own. To understand ourselves as leaders, we must attend to our relationship with authority as our ego is fundamentally shaped by this. This is what I will refer to in the next chapter as the imprint of authority.

We shall see that in reflecting in this way, another paradox emerges. That is, to truly be able to set our ego aside, we must first attend to its needs. Our defences often emerge as helpful survival responses to challenging situations. However, when we are no longer in those situations and they solidify over time into our personality or leadership approach, then they can become maladaptive. For example, if because of prior experiences, our sense of safety comes from being in control, we may go into 'fight mode' and slip into authoritarianism under stress. On the other hand, if our safety results from pleasing or pacifying others, we may try to bargain with or befriend those we lead. Furthermore, our fear response to a colleague or young person's anger may trigger a 'freeze', leading to a form of shut down which might be protective but is not constructive in a leadership role.

If we can work with these perfectly natural responses to stress rather than against them, we find the keys to a healthier and more empathetic way of working. The next chapter will suggest some tools to support you in developing your self-attunement. This a form of self-parenting that includes awareness of our own attachment and authority styles and the ways in which we inhabit these in our bodies and behaviours. Attuning to oneself in this way then leads to greater attunement and emotional availability in our interpersonal interactions (Siegal, 2012).

## Where to Begin

It starts with slowing down. Notice your breath and your body. 'Notice that' will be a recurring suggestion in the book. Paradoxically (once again), listening to our bodies and feelings rather than overriding them allows us not to be ruled by them.

Often our stress responses are preconscious. We might not be rationally aware of them. However, if we tune in, tension, pain and fear can be indications that something is wrong or needs to change. As Dan Siegal explains, 'When we pull away from pain, we actually make it worse. Moving towards a challenging feeling or situation helps us stay present' (Siegal, 2012, p. 286). By exploring pain and giving permission to what is difficult, we can release tension and find ways of being that are more aligned or, as Siegal describes it, 'integrated'.

What starts with the body can then be extended to other aspects of life. If we can engage with what is difficult – a challenging conversation with a colleague, the fear at the heart of a safeguarding case – rather than resisting it, we can ease the suffering just a little. It is what Kevin Hawkins explains in the following formula: suffering = pain × resistance (Hawkins, 2017). By finding a way to prevent our fearful or avoidant strategies from being activated and by sitting with what is difficult – what Dan Siegal describes as 'expanding the window of tolerance' – we are able to help bring resolution to painful non-integrated processes in our lives (*ibid,*) and in turn be more open to and for others.

## Mindfulness Practice

Whilst I have been clear from the outset that this is not a book about meditation, I think it is helpful to include a note on mindfulness practice at this point. Any leadership practice will be enriched by it. Research has shown mindfulness-based programs to be beneficial for adults' psychological health (Khoury et al., 2013), ability to manage stress (Chiesa & Serretti, 2009) attention and emotional balance (Sedlmeier et al., 2012). Many mindfulness-based programs have been developed specifically for teachers. Such programs aim to support teachers in developing 'habits of mind' (Roeser, Skinner, Beers, & Jennings, 2012, p. 167) so that they can create learning environments that are emotionally supportive whilst also maintaining their own well-being and motivation for teaching.

When we train in mindfulness, we train ourselves to encounter the present moment. Much of this is focused on the body. Western dualistic thinking likes to consider the mind separate to the body. (Barrett, 2021). However, many Eastern traditions, including Buddhism, recognise what Interpersonal Neurobiology is now proving empirically, that they are fundamentally interconnected. By consciously cultivating the connections between the mind and body, we can find greater balance in our everyday lives. For example, slowing our breathing makes us feel calmer, and feeling our feet on the floor helps us feel strong and supported. This simple practice is a rich resource for changing things, first of all for ourselves and then for others.

It is easy to say that there is no time for such practices, but as we shall explore, taking time to pause and reflect always pays dividends in terms of how we feel in ourselves, how we relate to others and our decision-making capacity. These practices do not have to be long and daunting. Having some time built at the beginning and end of the day to sit and sense rather than think, to be rather than do is hugely beneficial. The practice that follows is so simple and can be done anywhere: at your desk, on your commute, even in your classroom.

# Short Meditation to Support Yourself

- Find a comfortable seat.

- Sit up tall, use as many cushions or props to support you as you need and drop your shoulders.

- Put your hands in a comfortable place. Try one hand on your chest and one on your belly, or leave them both resting on your knees.

- Notice your breath. You do not need to force it; just watch it.

- Your mind will wander; that is okay. Just return to your breath.

- Remind yourself that in this moment, there is nothing to do and no one to be.

- Return to your breath.

- That is all.

Over time this practice can allow you to develop a rich reservoir of calm and support which you can draw from when things get difficult – as they inevitably will if you are a leader. When we 'get our own house in order' and are well resourced ourselves, we can really jump into our work in the way so many of us long to do. Freed from our own ego's fear and need to be approved of, we can be clear-headed enough to really prioritise what matters for those we serve. Then we will finally be able to be the adult in the room.

---

### Oli Knight Discusses his Approach to Leadership and Well-being

I had an epiphany as a Head of Department and Advanced Skills teacher at a school in special measures in Tower Hamlets back in 2006 or 2007. Those were the days when we were expected to provide written comments for every child and for them to respond to this marking. I taught 400 kids, which meant 400 comments every fortnight – insane. It was a big time of transition for me. I stopped doing anything else, I didn't go climbing, I didn't see my friends. It was a very one-dimensional experience. I said, 'Forget it. I'm never doing that again'. I realised that it didn't matter how hard I worked. I was never going to get it all done. So I realised you have to be sensible about your workload.

I have carried this with me into my third headship. I try really hard not to work all evening or on weekends. I know I could work seven days a week and still have work to do. It is because of this that I shouldn't expect anyone else to. We try really hard to have a system that shouldn't mean staff are working evenings and weekends. It doesn't always work and we can always get better, but that is the dream.

At my current school, we have tried to do small things that, added together, hopefully have a positive impact. For example, we have included meetings in a teacher's loadings. If you are a Main Scale teacher, you traditionally have a 30-period week with 10% PPA time, which is 27 periods a week of teaching. With us the maximum loading is 24. This is because our department meetings and two additional periods of intellectual preparation time are factored in. This is expensive resource wise but sets an important expectation. It elevates the value of the work that teachers do in this time. If meeting to discuss student work and plan a reteach is important, then it should be part of the school day, not a bolt-on.

Viviane Robinson (2011) has written an excellent paper on the impact of leadership on student outcomes, essentially on what heads should spend their time doing or resourcing. I think it is a safe bet that of all the things within the control of a head or a school, it is teachers that have the biggest impact on student outcomes. Therefore, we need to resource strategically with that in mind. That means making decisions about what you spend and don't spend money on. If you want teachers to spend more time reflecting on and improving their practice, talking through misconceptions before starting a new enquiry and planning and reteaching based on student error, you have to take things away.

- We don't do parents' evenings.

- We don't write comments in books.

- We don't produce written reports.

- We only assess and therefore enter data twice a year.

- We make maximum use of centralised curriculum materials so our staff are not spending 12 hours a week curating resources; they can use that time to better effect discussing as a team how to teach a certain topic, what the likely misconceptions might be within the topic and the best questions to pose to elicit those misconceptions.

- We've shifted a lot of the burden of assessment back onto the students. We use technology to track homework and quizzes. This is where tech really adds value in schools. In my opinion, it can't teach students the curriculum, but it can streamline administration and generate useful insights to aid a teacher's next steps with a class.

So we try to create systems that enable greater efficiencies where we can generate them and then use tech where it has a place. The other side of the coin, of course, is that fundamentally, this is a job. There is a whole world outside work that also deserves our attention. For me that often revolves around the question 'What type of parent do I want to be and what am I modelling to my own children?' I still struggle with the expectations now, but I must ask, what model do I want to set for them? I want them to have a work ethic and see that hard work opens doors, but I also want them to see that life is precious and there's loads to get done. However, I appreciate that this is a privileged position to take. In all these books on great leaders, the common theme is that everyone makes time for themselves. If you don't put oil in the lamp, eventually the lamp runs out.

So I try really hard to be flexible in supporting others to do this; I don't always get it right, but we do try. You can't measure it, but I'm sure if people don't feel aggrieved, they are more likely to tolerate other things. It has a minor impact on school but a big impact on the person. It creates flexibility in the system. People will be more willing to work hard in periods of stress and ride out the day-to-day rubbish, an extra period of cover, etc. That helps everyone. My philosophy is that provided the work is done, it doesn't matter when it's done. Workplaces must become more flexible. I see it with my partner and her career, and I don't want my own staff to go through the same issues as far as I can control this.

Part of the problem around well-being and school performance is, I am sure, down to the rhetoric that certainly existed when I was an NQT and in the early stages of my career. This notion is that you should sacrifice yourself on the altar of public service. No one is saying that the work is not vital and that teachers don't make a fundamental difference to a child's life, but we also have to live in the real world. The elephant in the room with teacher well-being – and it has been a resident for some time – is the complex relationship many teachers have with their professional life. I had the pleasure of doing some work with Professor David Hopkins a few years back, and he introduced me to this idea of the intertwining of personal and professional identities. The intricacy of these connections means that often a teacher sees their classroom as an extension of their personal identity. As a result, we often see feedback as a commentary on our personal self rather than our professional practice. This identity crisis weaves in a whole additional layer of stress to the role that needs to be unpacked carefully. We need to give ourselves permission to maintain our personal values and beliefs yet change our practice.

I think this relationship is something everyone struggles with in teaching, and we sometimes don't help ourselves with the culture we create in school. But I don't think it is the same in other professions, and we should shine a light on it. People often talk about the pressure of being a leader, and for sure there are pressures and it can be stressful, but this is in your control, and in my opinion, you have to do something to switch off and gain perspective. Everyone needs to have a hobby – something outside their professional life that nurtures and renews them. It's a great, rewarding job, but it shouldn't define you. It's not the most important thing; I think we get into trouble when we are consumed by our job and it squeezes out other things. I lie awake at night thinking about where I want to go climbing next. I wake up early every day to do 30 minutes of Pilates so I can feel ready for the day; I have a hang board at home (and in my office, which no one knows about!) and try to go to the climbing wall every other evening. I might end the day by doing a quick 30-minute HIT session in my office before going home – small things that help me recharge and decompress. I want to run a fantastic school, but I also want to look back on my life and have loads of great memories and experiences to recall. For me that is time with my family or time climbing, and to enjoy my time climbing, I have to be able to charge hard. Ultimately I don't think it really matters what it is, just that it is something.

My final thought would be that I think it is important to remember that good working conditions are not the same as allowing people to do bad work, and this often gets thrown at discussions around well-being or work-life balance. What we should be doing as leaders is creating the conditions, putting systems in place, to allow people to be really good, and part of that is picking people up who aren't doing the work to the standard required and supporting them to improve. The job of heads is to build great schools. This is the way to smash the nexus between background and achievement. It is up to us to create the conditions for people who are often really tired to do the best jobs they can. You get that by having great people in the building and doing everything you can to treat them well. You can't just wish for it; it has to be built. Part of this is giving people the right working conditions for them to be great.

It's complex work and I'm definitely no expert, but it's worth thinking more about.

## Summary

- Never has the need been greater for a more mindful way of leading our schools.

- To have a healthy and successful school culture, we need to make sure our schools **safe bases** that are free from fear.

- To do so, we need to prioritise **slowing** down, doing **one thing** at a time, **reflecting** and then **streamlining** to create yet more space.

- These things are not easy to do but **start with ourselves.**

- We are required to **set our ego aside** and attend to both the **emotional and logical** parts of our work and ourselves.

- We cannot do so without the right **resources**.

- Mindfulness practice has been shown to **improve attention** and **emotional balance** and can **support** us.

- It allows us to **see things more clearly**, be more empathetic and become better leaders.

# 2 **The Imprint of Authority**

This chapter will explore the following:

- The key tenets of attachment theory

- The role that attachment plays in our work as teachers

- Some questions to help understand your own attachment style

- Our brain's embodied response to stress

- An explanation of polyvagal theory, neuroception and introception

- How polyvagal theory might help us feel differently about our work

- An introception practice to explore our embodied stress responses

## The Missing Link

My teacher training spent plenty of time preparing me to deal with challenging behaviour. As a cohort, we perversely – and sometime competitively – celebrated horror stories of who had suffered the most abuse at the hands of their students. In contrast to a mental health or social work training, this education provided little space or guidance to explore what the impact of this might be on our own well-being. Nor did it support us to understand how our own vulnerability might affect what happened in the classroom. Phillip Riley suggests that this is not unique to my experience: 'Experienced teachers know the power of these emotions in the classroom, but they are usually overlooked in teacher education courses.' He goes on to say that 'without an understanding of the raw emotions involved in teaching and adequate training in how to look after oneself and the students during moments of intensity, teachers are placed into intensely emotional environments ill equipped' (Riley, 2011, p. 324).

DOI: 10.4324/9781003198482-4

It was not that there was a lack of preparations on relationships per se; much guidance was given on how to build relationships with students. It was just that this mostly involved how to engage with them around their interests, an approach that now seems rather short-termist – introducing, for example, a creative writing activity on *Love Island* or discussing the Arsenal result rather than using the joy of the subject as a gateway to a shared passion. Nonetheless, I would argue that the real omission was that relationships were conceived of in a unidirectional way. That is, the focus was getting the child 'on board', as opposed to actually relating to *them*. Moreover, what I, as an individual, brought to the table was considered irrelevant.

Parker J. Palmer, a teacher and author, suggests that this way of thinking is a result of a bias in Western discourse, which reduces teaching to a transactional and intellectual process (Palmer, 2017, p. 96). That is, learning is something that teachers do *to* students rather than that they create together. Like Riley he suggests that the teacher-student relationship is dyadic – that is, it flows two ways. If we are willing to look at our own experience of relationships in the classroom, there is a chance to gain self-knowledge and enrich the experience for both the student and the teacher. This work required to 'know thyself' is neither fluffy nor narcissistic but will serve us and our students well (Riley, 2011).

I am not suggesting that the role of the teacher or leader is the same as that of their students. Teacher expertise and authority are vital. And I do not mean that teachers are responsible for students' behaviour. Much of what happens in the classrooms is influenced by the culture and expectations of the school and the wider world as well, of course, as the individual choices of the students. We can acknowledge that we as teachers bring our moods and experiences into our work and that this affects the nature of our relationships without holding ourselves solely responsible. The conversation often lacks nuance. Unchecked, student-centred approaches can disempower students and lead to unrealistic expectations of teachers. Some excellent work has been done in recent years to rebalance the discourse and ensure that the expertise and authority of the adults in schools is respected, but this should never come at the expense of teacher reflection or humility.

To do this reflection, it is helpful to consider some approaches, which are drawn in under the umbrella of Interpersonal Neurobiology – namely attachment theory and polyvagal theory – in order to explore how an individual's own experiences might shape their classroom and leadership practices.

## Attachment Relationships

Riley proposes that an understanding of the human attachment system can shed light on classroom dynamics. (2011, p. 38). The proponents of attachment theory, Ainsworth and Bowlby (1991), suggested that attachment starts at birth, and it continues to impact health, well-being and relationships throughout life. An infant cannot survive without a parent, and thus, the goal of attachment is to keep the care seeker close to its caregiver. This act is referred to as its secure base. Babies have innate care-seeking behaviours – crying, gurgling, etc. – and respond power-fully to faces. Equally, adults respond to babies' need for proximity by attending to these behaviours. The care seeker will express separation protest if the distance between them becomes too great by crying, tantruming or bargaining. Whilst these behaviours are innate, the attachment bond is learnt through repeated exposure and is therefore unique to the environment and relationships in which it emerges (Riley, 2011, p. 13). The nature of this affectional bond influences how the baby forms other future relationships, what is termed the Internal Working Model (Ainsworth & Bowlby, 1991).

Ainsworth and Bowlby (*ibid.*) categorised attachment styles into secure and insecure attachment. From there, they further subcategorised insecure attachment types into anxious, avoidant and disorganised. In a secure attachment, the car-egiver is attuned to the child's needs and responds consistently and predictably. This results in an Internal Working Model of confidence in both itself and others. The caregiver provides boundaries, care and encouragement. They predict what the care seeker needs, making the world a safe and secure place to explore. This allows the child to gradually develop their own independence. Crucially, this does not have to be done perfectly. In order to develop self-efficacy, the caregiver intuits how and when to let the child struggle to achieve goals for themselves, what Winn-icott (2002) terms 'empathically failing the child'.

If a child has had to fend for themselves too much due to a lack of empathy or the situation the family finds themselves in, its explorations may become unful-filling or dangerous. As a result, the child learns not to venture out and will lose curiosity towards its environment. If the caregiver is rejecting or unavailable, a child will attempt to minimise their unmet needs in order not to experience the pain of separation. In later life, they may become distrustful of their own feelings and relationships with others and are more likely to become defensive to protect themselves from the pain of not having their needs met. This is termed 'insecure avoidant attachment' (sometimes referred to as 'dismissive' or 'defensive') and has serious implications for the child's cognitive and affective development (Riley, 2011, p. 511).

Anxious attachment, sometimes referred to as 'preoccupied', often occurs due to inconsistent or mis-attuned parenting. This can result in a fear of rejection, aban-donment or clinginess and has a powerful impact on an individual's relationships to themselves, their work and others.

If a child has a caregiver who is unpredictable, sometimes available, sometimes not, sometimes angry, sometimes loving, the child may take on characteristics of both the anxious and the avoidant attachment. This form of insecure attachment, later classified as 'disorganised attachment', can unleash unprecedented harm on a person's Internal Working Model. This is because it cannot function in a protective way by predicting caregiver behaviours. As a result, their sense of self and others may be particularly unsteady.

It is important to understand that separation protests are a normal rather than pathological response to environmental circumstances. Babies would very quickly die if left without a caregiver. However, separation behaviours can become maladaptive in new and safer environments. For example, the notable thing about an angry response born of separation anxiety is it is directed towards the attachment figure (Riley, 2011, p. 17). Whilst the function of this behaviour is to reduce the likelihood of the caregiver moving beyond a comfortable distance, it can also lead to the caregiver and care seeker becoming locked in an abusive dynamic. As a result, it may be difficult for a young person to have a 'corrective emotional experience' elsewhere. This is because the foundation on which other relationships are built is already insecure.

Maladaptive forms of separation protest include hypervigilance, aggression, clingy behaviours and freezing. Insecure attachments can have significant implications for the child's brain development and relationships. Abusive and neglectful attachment figures routinely predict violence in later life (Appleyard, Egeland, van Dulmen, & Alan Sroufe, 2005). Not only this, but this type of attachment can cause inordinate amounts of pain and challenges in an individual's relationships.

The primary attachment style asserts a powerfully robust influence on subsequent relationships. However, more recent research suggests that the Inner Working Model is not static and can in fact change through the lifespan (Kobak & Hazan, 1991; Scharfe & Bartholomew, 1994; Fonagy et al., 1996). This is good news for teachers as knowledge of attachment is a valuable tool for them to explain, predict and modify maladaptive separation behaviours.

## Attachment in School

School has the potential to provide young people such a corrective experience through peers and/ or teachers. However, many of the dynamics that fuel insecure attachment are also exacerbated in the school environment. In a student-teacher attachment dyad, many separations occur as a normal part of schooling. Whilst this is natural and beyond the control of both the student and teacher, each separation raises the possibility of separation anxiety, *and* each reunion provides opportunities for either a confirmatory or a corrective emotional experience (Riley, 2011, p. 15) – that is, either one that challenges the Internal Working Model or reconfirms it. If both parties are securely attached to both home and school, they find that separations are not permanent and that reunion can be a pleasure. This builds trust, self-efficacy and curiosity (*ibid.*). If the child is insecurely attached, it may be that they spend time anxiously awaiting or fearing the return to school. Or they may try to connect with the teacher as substitute attachment figure. Some of these behaviours may be more adaptive to the classroom setting than others. Insecurely attached students may need constant reassurance, or they may appear overly independent. Perhaps they settle well into routines but over time become rigid about following these rules and/or demonstrate reduced curiosity (*ibid.*), something that is vital for learning. On the other hand, they may be hypervigilant to threat and hierarchy. In the classroom, you might see a young person constantly turning around, responding to everything going on and/or seeking to assert themselves. Their anxiety could manifest itself in perfectionism, whereby they are never happy with themselves or their work and/or are constantly seeking the approval of the adults in the room.

That a school or individual teacher is able to offer opportunities for insecurely attached students to undergo corrective emotional experiences is extremely hopeful both for our student's happiness and well-being and their capacity to learn. However, this cannot happen if the teachers themselves are not secure. Despite population studies indicating that 30%–40% of people are insecurely attached, the impact of early experiences on how teachers approach their work is rarely dealt with in the educational literature (Riley, 2011). Discussions of attachment in school are often concerned with young people who have developed attachment disorders because of childhood trauma. However, leaders, teachers and students all have attachment needs.

Studies indicate that attachment style is responsive to the environment (Kobak & Hazan, 1991; Scharfe & Bartholomew, 1994; Fonagy et al., 1996). Even securely attached individuals behave in insecure ways in unsafe situations. Toxic school environments have the potential to make even the most secure teachers anxious or avoidant. However, good leaders also have the potential to extend corrective emotional experiences to their staff. Popper and Mayseless (2003) have explored the similarities between transformational leadership and good parenting. Sections Two and Three will draw on this notion to consider how we might make school a secure base for everyone to attach to. First, though, to know ourselves as leaders, we must consider how our own attachments histories impact our stress responses.

## Teacher Attachment

Phillip Riley's (2011) research suggests that attachment needs may have an impact on the motivation to become a teacher. An insecurely attached child tends to seek out substitute caregivers to provide a 'corrective emotional experience'. He proposes that if such a relationship happens to be with a teacher, it may influence a later decision to join the profession as part of a wish to help others achieve the same successful outcome. It is also possible that they may be seeking to repeat their experience of felt security by staying in the classroom. In this case, they would be looking to receive rather than give security. Whilst this is a thesis rather than a universal truth, it is interesting to think about how unmet attachment needs and separation protest on the part of the teacher might play out in the classroom. Then as teachers progress, if these needs continue not to be met, they might affect their leadership style.

Teaching is a high-stress and relentlessly relational profession with a unique set of vulnerabilities. Accountable to many masters, teachers operate at the 'dangerous intersection of public and personal life' (Palmer, 2017, p. 17) The teacher-student attachment relationship is complex. Teachers are caregivers to thirty-odd students, all with very different needs. But teachers also have their own needs.

Something both Palmer (2017) and Riley (2011) point to but which is rarely spoken about deserves some attention. Teachers have a uniquely vulnerable status in relation to their students. That is, a teacher needs their students to show a level of dependence on them for the teachers to construct and maintain their professional identity. Whilst most students may be willing to perform this, some, due to their experiences in or out of school, may not. The need for the respect (or even love) of young people to maintain our status and identity is the unconscious backdrop to every classroom, and so is the fear of losing it and of being exposed to their indifference, ridicule or judgement. From an attachment point of view, this puts the teacher in the role of care seeker as well as caregiver (Riley, 2011).

As Palmer says, 'Many of us became teachers for reasons of the heart, animated by a passion for some subject and for helping people learn' (Palmer, 2017, p. 17). However, because of this daily act of vulnerability, which we are not adequately prepared for or supported in, many lose heart. He puts it aptly when he says the following:

> I need not reveal personal secrets to feel naked in front of a class. I need only parse a sentence or work a proof on the board while my students doze off or pass notes. No matter how technical my subject may be, the things I teach are things I care about – and what I care about helps define my selfhood.

Teaching and leadership (in particular) are vulnerable professions. If we do not handle ourselves with care, then much like a child without good-enough caregiving, our ego creates survival strategies to protect us, some of which are counterproductive.

## Defences

Where we are driven by a fear of our own ineptitude, the ego strives to make our performance slicker. We cover up and show off. These defences show themselves in many ways, whether that is putting up barriers in relationships or focusing our attention on evidencing progress for an external observer. The result of this focus on performance is that our students and the teams that we lead learn to do the same (Palmer, 2017), be that copying each other's homework, cramming for tests or putting on a show for a lesson observation. Riley argues that by behaving in this way, we 'ironically, may limit the chances of teachers and students developing the kinds of relationships that foster better learning, which would reduce the need to be defensive' (Riley, 2011, p. 46).

Our defences particularly come up when we are threatened. When our relationships with our students, colleagues or other stakeholders are not secure, schools can become scary places. This fear might play out in our leadership and in the classroom in different ways. I will suggest some patterns of the insecure leader. They are stereotypes, but I am sure we have all seen them in our colleagues at some point, or perhaps we even see echoes of them in ourselves.

## Insecure Leadership Patterns

The insecure leader might be an 'authoritarian' who desperately needs to control their environment at all costs. Their approach is 'Do as I say, not as I do'. They require absolute control of their students and staff. This is not because that is the most effective environment for learning but because anything else would threaten their sense of self. They feel they must be in charge to be safe, and when triggered, they may become aggressive and find it difficult to back down.

Equally, though, an insecure leader may pursue love and approval from their colleagues or students. In seeking this, they may position themselves either as a 'mate' or as a 'charismatic leader'. They find separation or rejection from their staff or students a particular challenge. The charismatic leader uses their personality to draw students or colleagues in and can build amazing relationships. However, being all things to all people is ultimately an unobtainable goal. Not only does this make life difficult for other staff by setting up unreasonable expectations, but in the end, they either burn themselves out or let people down. It is much better to build consistency and share the load. Classically, the 'mate' also desperately wants to be liked by the students and so tries to befriend them. Depending on how interesting they are to the children, they may fall flat on their face, or their approach might have a modicum of success in getting them on their side – that is, until much like the *Love Island* strategy discussed earlier, the students realise that they are not actually their mate at all. This either comes about because the teacher challenges them to think outside of their current experience and pushes them to do work or because they get frustrated with not being listened to and finally assert the boundaries with the child.

These teachers may seek to befriend their students or those they lead but then become volatile if they are rejected or if the relationship is not completely on their terms. Perhaps this character, who wants to be liked by but also be in control of those they are responsible for, is the most challenging one. It presents the same difficulties for a child as 'disorganised parenting' would. This inconsistency can be very jarring for young people and adults alike, particularly those with insecure attachment themselves who need to maintain the integrity of their Inner Working Models at all costs.

## Know Thyself

In all of these personas, the Internal Working Model (or ego) is influenced by our early experiences. Whether the teacher or leader wants to be liked, idolised or in control, they are playing out a set of separation protests that have resulted from a unique set of circumstances. This is very human, and teachers are first and foremost human. Even the most privileged of us will have faced some adversity. This shapes the way we seek out safety in both positive and negative ways. My intention is not to shame leaders for not being perfect nor pathologise those who have unresolved trauma. Quite the opposite – if we can begin to think of teachers (us) as a people with needs, we can start to have compassion for ourselves. This in turn allows us to be attuned to and compassionate for those we lead.

It is helpful to stop and reflect on where our own experiences and defences might place us in relation to the insecure archetypes. You may recognise echoes of yourself in the 'authoritarian', 'charismatic leader' or 'mate'. Whilst this insight into our own vulnerability as teachers might be confronting, this self-knowledge is a gift. Through acknowledging our histories and being honest about the fact that we all have the need to feel safe and secure, we can start to examine with compassion who we are in our leadership, and then we can begin to find the tools to do it differently. As we come to know and accept our own vulnerabilities, they no longer have to rule us. Through gentle awareness, or mindfulness, we can explore our own triggers and reflect on how we might also trigger others. In doing so, we move towards a healthier persona, that of the mature adult. A secure leader is one who holds boundaries with love, respects the child's or colleague's autonomy and is not overidentified with them. They are one who wants the best for their staff and students but does not *need* anything back from them for their own validation. They know that whilst they are not perfect, they do not need to be; they are already enough.

It is likely that this will never be a fully finished project, and it does not need to be. It is difficult to be the secure adult day in and day out, particularly in an education system that does not support its leaders well. Nonetheless, resourcing yourself by holding your inner insecure child with love and understanding is a great place to start.

Self-knowledge is the first part of this. Understanding how our own attachment experiences affect our relationships, our expectations, the meaning we attribute to things and our responses is a useful step. The aim is not to become egoless but to begin to understand where you go when under stress and the habits and patterns that play out so you can track yourself and start to bring yourself back to a more mindful place. This is much like how, in a meditation practice, when you mind invariably starts to wander, you bring yourself back to noticing your breath.

George et al. (1985) created the Adult Attachment Interview.[1] I have adapted this as a starting point to consider your experiences and how this might shape your relationship with authority in the classroom (and in your leadership).

## Reflection Tool

Find a quiet space, and answer the following questions in your journal or diary. There are no right answers; just be open to what arises. Not every question may offer an insight, and those that do may come in ways that surprise you.

1 How would you describe your relationships with your parents or caregivers?

2 When you were upset or hurt physically as a child, whom would you go to?

3 What are your memories of separation in childhood?

4 Were your parents or caregivers ever threatening in any way? If so, how?

5 How do you feel your relationships with your parents or caregivers have affected your adult personality? Is there anything that held you back or has had a negative effect?

6 Were there any other adults to which you were close or who have had a significant impact on who you have become?

7 Did you experience the loss of a parent or close loved one as a child? Have you lost other close people during your adult years? How has this affected you?

8 What kind of relationships do you tend to have with your students?

9 Is there anything in particular that you have learnt from your childhood that impacts you in the classroom?

10 How would you describe yourself as a teacher?

11 Could you describe example positive and negative relationships?

12 Are there any particular students that you will never forget?

13 Do you ever dream about your students?

14 If you lead adults, how would you describe your leadership style?

15 How do you respond under stress, including in the classroom?

16 What are your 'triggers', and what calms you down?

## Body Budgeting

This form of self-reflection can be helpful for understanding the roots of some of our patterns of behaviour. However, if we really want to interrupt the more maladaptive dynamics at play in our relationships, we also need to engage with the embodied, relational and intuitive nature of the attachment system. To understand this process, it is helpful to explore the neurobiology a little.

Rationality and emotions are not at war (Barrett, 2021). Feldman Barrett's influential new book *Seven and a Half Lessons About the Brain* (2021) debunks the notion of the tripartite brain. That is that the neocortex, responsible for rational thinking, has evolved subsequently to the parts of the brain (reptile and mammal) responsible for our impulses and emotions.

Feldman Barrett suggests that rather than pure cognition, rationality might be better thought of in terms of body budgeting. Emotions can be extremely rational – for example, feeling afraid because you are in imminent danger. The rush of cortisol (a stress hormone) that prepares you to fight or flee in such a situation is actually our brain making a sound investment for our own survival. Even if you know there is no danger, such a stress response might still be rational when you frame it as body budgeting. Depending on someone's prior experiences, a fight-or-flight response might be very reasonably predictive and protective. Feldman Barrett cites the example of a soldier in a warzone, where threats would appear on a regular basis. In this case, not only would it be appropriate for the soldier to frequently predict the threats. Even if some turn out to be a false alarm because being on a high level of alert would be advantageous in keeping them safe – a sort of 'better safe than sorry' approach.

Of course, when one is no longer in a warzone, this response would become maladaptive. Feldman Barrett suggests that mental illness can be understood as body budgeting that is out of sync with the environment. If we think about the level of violence that some young people that we work with witness at home or on the street, rates of mental illness start to make sense. What is more, chronic levels of stress also have a significant impact on physical health and the capacity to learn and build relationships. Short-term surges of cortisol are no problem. However, over time these withdrawals from the body's budget – water, salt, glucose, etc. – take a toll. Thus, our relationships, our sense of safety, capacity to concentrate and learn new things and the choices we make are bound up with our physical and mental health (Siegal, 2012, p. 103).

So how does body budgeting link to the attachment system? Humans are a deeply social species. All mammals need some form of attachment to their caregiver for their survival. For human babies, the period of vulnerability is much longer. In fact, we do not have a fully formed adult brain until way into our twenties. That explains a thing or two, right? As a result of this, the stakes in our relationships are extremely high. There is a powerful wiring that mobilises our literal fear of annihilation when, as an infant, we are not close to our caregivers. As we grow, these same brain processes are activated when our Internal Working Model, formed to protect these relationships at all costs, is endangered.

If our attachment system is threatened, our flight-flight-freeze system becomes activated. This activation usually mobilises our sympathetic nervous system (see Figure 2.1) to respond to the threat (or perceived threat). Our defence is to either fight or run away. However, depending on the history and situation, our parasympathetic nervous system may become activated, and we may become immobilised. Just think of a mouse 'playing dead' in the jaws of a cat.

## Autonomic Nervous System

The autonomic nervous system is responsible for automatic control of your body functions. It has three branches:

1 The **sympathetic nervous** system is activated in response to stress. It controls *'fight or flight'* responses.
2 The **parasympathetic nervous system** is activated during calm times and is often considered the *'rest and digest'* or *'feed and breed'* system. It promotes growth and energy storage.
3 The **enteric nervous system** controls the gastrointestinal system.

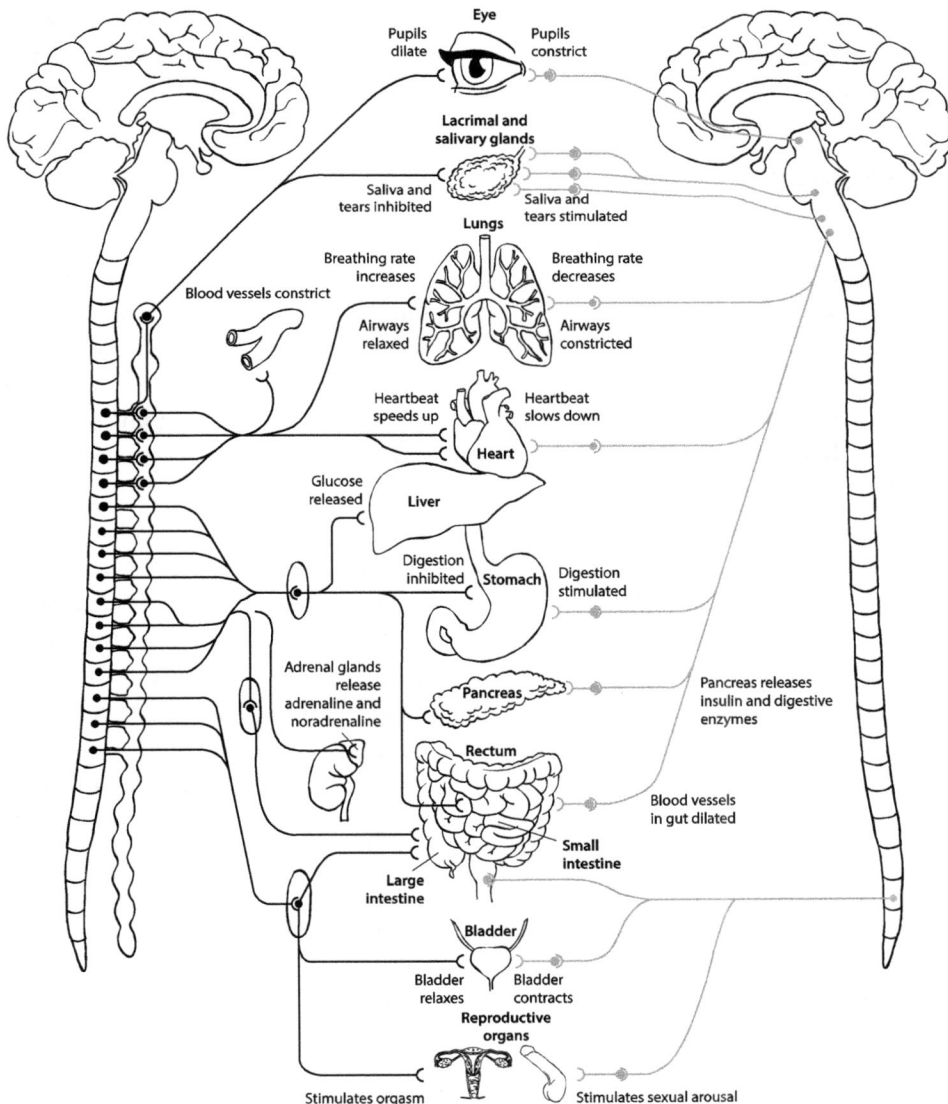

**Figure 2.1** The autonomic nervous system

*Source*: Reprinted with permission from psychologytools.com

## Fight, Flight, Freeze in School

It is helpful to think about how these processes might play out in schools. The 'authoritarian' teacher that shouts or squares up to the students who are not doing what they are asked could be characterised as demonstrating a 'fight defence'. The fear that teachers (particularly new ones) might have of getting back in the classroom, characterised by heart beating, sweating, shallow breathing – whether that is after a difficult lesson or a long holiday – could be viewed as a symptom of a flight response. Furthermore, the perceived apathy of some experienced colleagues to students' misbehaviour as they plough on with their lesson despite what is happening or the leader that closes the office door and buries their head in a spreadsheet whilst chaos ensues in the corridor could be conceived of as a form of freeze – what is referred to by Dr Stephen Porges, the proponent of polyvagal theory (2017), as a *dorsal-vagal* shutdown.

## Neuroception

Our subconscious ability to detect and respond to threat is termed 'neuroception' by Porges (2017). Our responses are not voluntary, and as a result, we may not be fully aware of our motivations or in a position to 'think our way out of it'. It is not simply a 'head brain' process. The brain is connected to the rest of the body's vital organs via the vagus nerve. As a result, mental processes are accompanied by embodied experiences – the quickening of the heart rate, the shortening of breath and even sometimes an evacuation of the bowels. It's literally a 'gut feeling'.

Understanding neuroception can bring clarity to a previously confusing set of responses, feelings and impulses and allow us to have compassion for ourselves and others. Porges describes his own experience of neuroception whilst having an MRI scan (Porges, 2017, p. 67). He explains that, as a scientist, he was intrigued by the process, which he knew to be very safe. Before undertaking the scan, he described feeling comfortable and not at all anxious. Yet when the platform moved under the MRI magnet, he felt compelled to ask the technician to pause so he could have glass of water. When they resumed the process, no sooner had his nose reached the core of the scanner when he said, 'I can't do this. Get me out'. In his own words, he 'couldn't deal with the confined space; it triggered a panic attack' (*ibid.*). What this serves to illustrate is that there are certain cues, often unique to us, that our nervous system detects as a threat. When our defences are triggered, we can become mobilised (or immobilised) whether or not we want to be. The lack of awareness or intention is key here. As Porges puts it, 'Perception requires a conscious awareness, while neuroception occurs reflexively without awareness' (*ibid.*).

The difficulty is, if we are constantly in a hypervigilant, self-protective state, it is likely that we will either seek unhealthy connection or push connection away altogether. To preserve the integrity of the internal working model, we invite more of what we are expecting. In order to move beyond this, Porges suggests that we need to work with the body and invite cues that signal safety to our nervous system. Paradoxically, this provides possibilities to consciously shape our behaviour. Importantly, though, it is not so much mind over body as bringing awareness to the body's processes in order to not be ruled by them.

## Introception

Developing self-understanding involves more than the intellectual capacity to reflect on what we have experienced in the past. Though this is important, we also need to learn to be open to whatever arises in our sensory world – the signals of our bones and limbs, the feedback from the organs of the torso. They, too, are valuable sources of information. As Bessel Van Der Kolk (2015) reminds us, the body does indeed *keep the score*.[2] In Interpersonal Neurobiology, this openness and awareness of the body's physical experience is termed 'introception'.

Through active introception – which mindfulness, dance, yoga, qi gong, prayer and many other forms of meditative practice can all cultivate – we can gain a deep sense of connection to ourselves, a bodily sense of being alive. This also allows us to be more deeply connected to others because if we are calm, the nonverbal signals that we project are perceived and processed by others as safe, allowing them in turn to resonate with us.

For many of us, that our nervous systems are connected to others in a physiological sense might seem a bit wacky. However, on reflection, it really makes a lot of sense. We appraise each other's body language and tone constantly, seeking to understand where it is safe to build connection and where to step back. Does this person want a hug or a handshake? Even more so in times of pandemic. We notice if someone looks withdrawn and think perhaps something is bothering them. We read whether it is appropriate to intervene or give them space. This impacts us too. When someone is warm and welcoming, we feel safe and relaxed. When someone shouts or there is an incongruency between their words and our felt experience, we tense up.

As we shall see in Section Three, being aware of what we communicate through our bodies in the classroom matters. Some simple shifts in manner can make a big difference for our students. For now, though, let us consider how our experiences at work might be impacting our own nervous system through a simple introception practice.

## Introception Practice

This practice is best done in a quiet, private space. It will help you to explore through your imagination what your embodied stress responses might be. You may want to investigate your experience of a place (the playground, the corridors, the classroom, the assembly hall) or a situation (a whole staff meeting, teaching 8B, coaching a colleague), or it may be an individual relationship (with a particular task, colleague, parent, student, even an Ofsted inspector). It is about exploring with openness and curiosity what arises in your body. There is no requirement to judge it or need to change it (that will come). Simply acknowledging it, being with it and perhaps sending your breath there is enough.

- Find a comfortable seat. Start by imagine yourself doing that thing with that person in that space/situation. This is an enquiry, so remember to be non-judgemental of yourself.

- Feel your feet on the floor. How are you supporting yourself? Is your weight evenly balanced? Are you giving your full weight into the floor or holding tension further up in your body? Sit with your back away from the back of the chair if possible.

- Notice how your body feels in general. How safe do you feel? Is there an inclination to move towards or away from the situation?

- Enquire into this feeling. What qualities is it imbued with? Is there a tendency to want to control that person or situation or to fawn in front of it or be dominated in some way? Do you feel you want to be mobilised or immobilised?

- Now scan through your body. You can put a hand between the bottom of your ribs and your navel. Notice your breath, where the movement is in your body. Is it in your chest? Your belly? Are there parts of you that are frozen or tense? Are your shoulders or upper body collapsed?

- Next, notice your face – your forehead, jaw, tongue and teeth. Is there a natural sense of a smile? Is there a sense of tension in your jaw, cheeks or forehead? Do your eyes feel strained or relaxed? As much as is bearable, feel the points of tension rather than resisting them and breathe.

- What about your shoulders? Notice if there is any tension in your shoulders or neck? Are they open or closed? Hunched or relaxed? Is your centre of gravity forward or backwards? Again, feel into any points of tension and breathe.

- What about your hands? Are you ready to fight and defend yourself? Is there a tendency to make a fist? Or are your hands open and welcoming? Notice this without judgement and breathe.

- Then explore below the diaphragm. We feel things here when we are anxious. Feel your belly and gut (it can help to put your other hand there). What is going on? Do things feel relaxed? Is there gurgling? Notice without shame or judgement. Do you feel tense or bloated or a little queasy? Do you have butterflies or the need to go to the toilet?

- Now, bring your attention to the whole of your body once more to finish.

This practice can become both a source of information and a tool to fight back with when we are on 'automatic pilot'. You may like to practise it regularly in moments where you are relaxed or when you are more tense. The more you practice, the easier it will become. Using intention and focused attention in this way, we can gather information and analyse from an open and curious place what is happening inside ourselves. From here we can begin to explore what we can do to remedy it.

## Choice and Change

Reflecting on these processes can create choice and change. Interestingly, improved functioning of the prefrontal cortex is an outcome measure of both mindfulness practice and a secure parent-child attachment. This is not the rational part of the brain somehow dampening down our emotional responses. It is not *mind over body* but a process of integration. Welcoming knowledge of the relationship between our emotions, physical sensations and thinking processes can help us to make different choices and invite signals of safety to regulate and recentre our nervous systems.

Mindfulness, yoga and other forms of meditative practice are ways to do this. It is not about having nice abs or being a 'good meditator' but creating space to be present and respond empathetically to whatever arises in yourself. The literature suggests that inner reflection involves a form of internal attunement (Siegal, 2012, p. 69).

Secure parent-child attachment is characterised by interpersonal attunement, a form of communication that involves a parent attending to the child's needs in an open and kind way. So to feel safe and think clearly, we need to parent ourselves.

This matters; it supports us to prevent our insecurities leaking out onto those we teach and lead and resources us so we do not burn out. Some strategies for integrating this into our lifestyles will be explored in the next chapter on self-care.

## Summary

- Interpersonal Neurobiology offers an understanding of how our **mind, body and relationships are interconnected**.

- Attachment theory and polyvagal theory help to explain how our **early experiences** and sense of **felt security** structure our **patterns of relating** to the world.

- If we are met with **coregulation**, then there are possibilities for these patterns to change through **'corrective emotional experiences'** that literally 'rewire' the brain.

- **Teachers and leaders** are first and foremost people, and they therefore have **attachment needs**, including the need to feel safe and supported in their school.

● If we are in an **insecure environment** or have had challenging early experiences, we may **unintentionally trigger** and be **triggered** in our work.

● By attending to our attachment **history** and the **feedback from our bodies** (introception), we can become more **mindful and attuned** to **ourselves** and in turn **in our leadership**.

## Notes

1 Reproduced with permission from University of California, Berkeley.
2 The title of Bessel Van Der Kolk's bestselling 2015 book is *The Body Keeps the Score: Mind, Brain and Body in the Transformation of Trauma.*

# 3 Self-Care

This chapter will explore the following:

- The notion of a healthy mind platter to support us with a balanced lifestyle
- The role of rest and downtime, reflection and joy in well-being
- How these can be built into school life
- A practice to 'hold yourself' when things are difficult

I have learnt the hard way that taking responsibility for your own well-being is not an optional extra. As leaders, we have a moral imperative to look after ourselves. Even if you can get by in the short term on adrenaline or caffeine, this is not an effective long-term strategy. Furthermore, as described in the previous chapter, we resonate interpersonally, so when we are stressed, we 'leak'. It is at risk of labouring the point, but it feels important to stress that self-care is a paradox. The better you support yourself, the more able you are to support others. However, this is not the intention in and of itself; you are also just deserving of it!

Moreover, I hope this chapter will serve to illustrate that self-care goes far beyond taking bubble baths – though they can be exceptionally effective after a difficult day or even at the start if things are that bad. Instead, it speaks to the heart of what it means to live a more mindful life. When we recognise our wholeness and humanity, we accept that not only are we not automatons but we also would not want to be. Teaching is a fundamentally interpersonal endeavour, and that is why it is so exhausting but also so rewarding and transformational.

## The Healthy Mind Platter

Routines, or rhythms, have a role to play in keeping us healthy. Much like the sound of our heartbeats, our daily, weekly or yearly practices keep us in check and make the world a safe and predictable place. They allow us to get into positive habits and achieve things that we could not have done without the structure. We

DOI: 10.4324/9781003198482-5

recognise this easily in children. I will explore the role of routine in the classroom in Section Three, but it really is no different for adults.

Siegal describes good mental health as integration. That is the sweet spot between chaos and rigidity (2012). He introduces us to the notion of the healthy mind platter. Riffing on the familiar image of the healthy food plate that reminds us of what we should eat each day, he suggests that there are seven mental activities that are important to make time for to introduce balance and well-being into our days and lives.

His framework (Siegal, 2012, pp. 293–294) for a balanced mental health 'diet' is the following:

1  Focus time: closely paying attention

2  Play time: activities that are spontaneous, playful and creative

3  Connecting time: joining with other people and with nature

4  Physical time: moving the body, aerobically if possible

5  Time in: reflecting inwardly on sensations, images, feeling and thoughts

6  Down time: The non-goal-directed focus of open attention

7  Sleep time

With this notion of balance in mind, I think it is important to emphasise that the aim of routine is not control and rigidity but in fact greater resilience and flexibility. Routines are a means to an end, not an end in themselves. 'Rhythm' is perhaps a more helpful term as it frees us from the connotations of control. With this in mind, I would suggest saying no to dour lifestyles and clean eating and saying yes to moderation and enjoyment of life in balance. Furthermore, what works for one might not work for another, which is why Siegal's principles are so helpful. We all need to find our 'middle way'.

## Rest

Though none of Siegel's suggestions are rocket science, our busy lifestyles have moved us so far away from this common sense that the reminders to connect, play, take downtime and sleep feel very welcome. In a world that drives efficiency and schedules every waking moment, this approach acknowledges the need for time to *be* rather than just to *do*.

For those of us who are hyper-organised, it can be hard to give ourselves permission to find the time for this. My tip is to (somewhat paradoxically) schedule it in and ensure a little bit of down time every day.

Watching TV does not really count. Porges (2017) explains why; when we attend to computer monitors, we are 'basically recruiting a hypervigilant state that is slightly modified to provide a state of focused sustained attention. This is not a state that supports health, growth, and restoration, nor does it support the social engagement behaviours necessary for successful social interactions' (2017, p. 235).

Reading, taking a bath (damn, I mentioned it), playing games (not computer-based ones) and talking with good friends or loved ones are some good examples of non-goal-oriented time. However, all of these can become goal oriented if you let them. It requires a mindset shift. There is nothing to achieve. Meditation can help with this.

Dr Nerina Ramlakhan, author of *Tired but Wired* (2010), points out that we no longer incorporate switch-off moments into our days. Our society is restless. This leads to a constant desire for us to multitask, which means that our minds are kept busy right up until when we go to bed at night. It is no wonder then that so many of us find it difficult to sleep. In a world that valorises efficiency and busyness, recognising the role of downtime and sleep feels like a radical act.

Of course, when you rest, there are also tangible benefits to yourself and others, including again, paradoxically, your efficiency. Sleep integrates learning from the day and consolidates memory. In her fabulous book *Why I'm No Longer Talking About Wellbeing* (2020), Kat Howard reminds us of the futility of working too late. Most of us do not do our best work at night, nor are we any good to others when we are exhausted. She cites Professor Russell Foster of the University of Oxford, who states that when you lack sleep, 'your ability to make rational decisions fails and you become impulsive. . . . You lack empathy and your social interactions will also be compromised' (2020, p. 46).

Even if we are tired, it is not always easy to sleep. A routine can really help. Howard suggests that to prepare yourself for sleep, you should 'set an alarm or reminder 15 minutes before you want to aim to be in bed. Close the laptop down, brush your teeth, have a skincare routine – all of those things that we rush to do at the end of the night can be done with the time that you have allowed yourself' (Howard, 2020, p. 47). I wind myself down like you would a small child – avoiding screens, keeping the noise and lights quiet, not eating too late, having a bath and reading a story (to myself).

Reorienting ourselves towards the importance of sleep and downtime requires a shift in perspective, one that accepts we do not always need to be 'on', that good things can occur when we rest and turn inward. Katherine May's (2020) concept of *wintering* is an interesting one, I think. She suggests, 'We must learn to invite the winter in. . . [and] engage with it mindfully, even to cherish it' (May, 2020, p. 12). Once we start to think of things more in terms of rhythms and cycles or outward expansions and inner contractions, we begin to see them everywhere and how integral they are to good health. This is obvious in the cycles of the natural world. Consider a tree that loses its leaves in the autumn. Those leaves decay and feed both the tree and the rest of the ecosystem. Whilst the tree is almost dormant in the winter, the sap will rise again, ready for the spring. As we, too, are part of nature, it is important to recognise how our energy functions in a similar way.

The more we attune to our bodies, the more we can understand our own rhythms and cycles, whether they are daily, monthly, yearly or over a lifespan. Research indicates that it is not just women who have hormonally driven cycles (Diamond, 2004). However, people who menstruate need to be especially attuned to what they can and cannot do at certain times of the month. I have learnt to reframe my menstrual and premenstrual time, not as a time of weakness but as *time in*, to stop and reflect – something that makes me wiser and stronger in the long run. This is of course the way all good growth and learning happens, with outward time to learn and inward time to consolidate. Taking *time in* will also guide you as to what you need. It allows you to reflect on what tires you and what frees up energy, helping you focus on the things that matter. This is really what it means to lead mindfully.

## Reflection

In keeping with the seasonal metaphor, the tools in Chapter 2 can be used for an 'emotional spring clean'. This 'cleanliness' can be maintained through a level of (gently) disciplined routine in your life. Building in regular space for reflection is key. This can be done in several ways. I personally find that a brief (no more than ten minutes) sitting meditation first thing in the morning and last thing at night sets me up well for the day and helps me wind down at night. I also get on well with 'morning pages', a notion that Julia Cameron (1992) introduces in her now infamous book *The Artist's Way*. She suggests writing three (though I often do two) pages of stream-of-consciousness writing when you wake up in the morning. It is not so much as writing as a form of expression, of clearing away thoughts and worries so you can be more conscious and present in your day.

However, there are numerous other ways to journal that support both reflection and organisation. They do not have to be a free flow of consciousness or a Pinterest-worthy bullet journal. It could be making good use of tech by synching up diaries and devices. The important thing is that you find what works for you.

## A Balanced Lifestyle

The space that is created through this reflection can then be applied to maintaining simplicity and balance in different areas of your life. Limiting screen time, social media and news consumption in particular has been important for me. Likewise, so does reducing alcohol and other substances (sugar and caffeine very much included).

A healthy mind platter should of course be accompanied by a healthy diet and an active lifestyle. Looking after and respecting your body looks different for different people. It might mean giving in to treats more often, or it might involve introducing more healthy foods and a bit of discipline. What you eat effects your mood, but your mood also affects how and what you are able to digest. Exposure to stress leads to alterations of the brain-gut interactions, leading to the development of a broad array of gastrointestinal disorders, including food intolerances (Konturek, Brzozowski, & Konturek, 2011). I know this from personal experience of being able to eat whatever I want on holiday and then suffering terrible IBS in term time.

In my humble opinion, eating plenty of plants that are fresh, local, seasonal and organic, where possible, whilst also making sure you have enough of what you enjoy (if veg does not float your boat) in moderation is the key to a truly balanced diet. There are of course environmental reasons to go more plant-based and organic too. More and more studies are indicating how our physical and mental well-being are linked to the health of the planet (Hamilton et al., 2021).

Go outdoors. A large-scale study by Exeter University found that spending at least two hours a week was a crucial threshold for health and well-being (Whitworth, 2019). The Japanese practice of *shinrin yoku*, forest bathing, is one simple and mindful way with proven benefits. It simply involves observing nature and breathing deeply.[1]

Drink plenty of water. I heard Kathrine Birblisingh, head of Michela Community School, talk about how she only drinks water and herbal tea throughout the school day, avoiding all caffeinated drinks. Whatever you think of her political and pedagogical persuasions, it is hard to deny that she is clear-headed and energised. I try to do the same. At the very least, I make sure water is the first thing I drink in the morning (warm with some lemon is particularly good for the system).

There seems to me no more damning indictment of how unentitled we feel to attend to our body's most basic needs than Howard's research, which indicates that many teachers drank less water at school purposefully to avoid taking time out to go to the toilet (2020, p. 40). I know of too many teachers who get repeated UTIs as a result. She cites a study which says that nearly three-quarters of teachers say their workload is having a serious impact on their physical health (*ibid.*). Chronic back pain is another common issue, as Howard again notes. 'In most other professions, there is an HR department to ensure that you have an ergonomically acceptable desk setup, but in teaching we make do with broken chairs, the sofa in the staff room, shaky monitors and/or broken laptops. If we continue to shovel food in our months crammed over our computers or absentmindedly whilst we are on duty, then many of us will continue to suffer from crippling IBS and other digestive issues. And what else can we expect? Our bodies need time (and mindfulness) to eat, rest and digest properly. As Howard says, 'We push a little harder, for a little longer, and can forget that, in doing so, we are sabotaging ourselves a little in the process' (Howard, 2020, p. 45).

How might you realistically build some of this into your busy working life? Again, Howard has some great ideas. She suggests thinking about the daylight you have access to at work. She points to the impact of spending much of your day in environments that lack windows or without access to fresh air might have on your sleep and physical health. I know that on some winters, arriving and leaving in the dark, I would not see daylight until the weekend – horrific. Find 15 minutes to walk during the working day, or just eat lunch outside. There are ways to do this. It can be lovely to eat in the canteen with colleagues and students. It provides an opportunity to be social, to be visible, to build relationships and to be in an environment that is not your office or classroom. But taking quiet time for yourself during the school day is also very valid. Could this be done in a quiet corner of the playground or a nearby park? Howard also suggests standing to teach and, when sitting, being mindful of your posture. The benefits for your and your students' strong and aligned physical stance are manifold. Section Three will consider this further.

## Joy

Finally, to return to Siegal's platter, it is important to make time for play and have fun. This is not only enjoyable but also good for our well-being. In fact, the two are totally interconnected. Well-being has become another dreary thing to *do*. As the inimitable psychiatrist Dr Clare Short advised a group of sixth-form leavers recently, 'Forget about well-being, make time for doing what you enjoy' (2021).

Porges (2017) explains the role of reciprocal play in recruiting the social engagement system, which is extremely important for the normal functioning of the body, supporting our enthusiasm, motivation and digestion amongst other things. Play also allows us to try things out in safe ways, allowing for more creative responses. On a neurological level, our brains are able to try out new firing patterns when we play, increasing our neuroplasticity and literally helping to rewire our brains. Crucially, though, this play should not be solo. Porges' research indicates that solitary play is something different, self-soothing. Whilst it also has an important function, it does not bring the social engagement system online. A Longitudinal Harvard study by Grant & Glueck[2] is clear: relationships are the most important factor in health.

## Relationships

Therefore, who you surround yourself with at home and at work matters. Is it helpful to ask yourself who nourishes you? Where do you feel felt and seen? Who am I able to play and be myself? Establishing support networks and mentors that inspire your growth is key. Remember that number one on Siegal's list is *focus time*. Ensuring that we are learning and have a sense of purpose matters for our motivation and well-being. In Sections Two and Three, we will consider this in relation to the culture of learning that we might create in the classroom and in the wider school.

However, it is all about balance. It is necessary to have friends with whom you do not discuss work and with whom you can explore and nourish different parts of yourself too.

# A Caveat

Now of course none of this is easy to make happen if you are forced to take work home. You are much more likely to reach for the sugar, the caffeine or the alcohol if you have just had an exhausting lesson, day or week. The guidance to 'park your ego at the door' or prioritise 'self-care' can sound insensitive when there is just so much to do. This is particularly apparent in toxic institutions, where fear – the threat of league tables, Ofsted, parental complaints, I could go on – drive the culture, and it often feels like we have no choice but to work in the way that we do.

One side effect of the secularisation of mindfulness, away from the more religious or communal ethic of Buddhism, is that it has become overly focused on the individual. Whilst I am making the case to start with yourself, I am not suggesting that it is *all* on you. Nor should we be gung-ho about opening ourselves up when we are not ready or are in environments that are not safe. The ego has a necessary protective function. If you are in a high-stakes environment that judges you on your performance, going against the grain in ways that this book will suggest could make you dangerously vulnerable. I know from my own experience that trying to change culture to make it feel safe for others to be honest and creative and to fail, in an environment which was fundamentally not safe for me, was impossible.

There are times when what is needed is to do the deep work, changing yourself first so that you can create a better environment for others. However, there are also times that you just need to get out and find an environment that you are better supported in. Part of leading mindfully is having the discernment and courage to know which is needed and then act on it. There is no shame in seeking help or moving to a more supportive environment. We cannot change our institutions through individual personal reflection alone; culture is key. That involves other people too.

Ultimately, your own self-care has to be held in a broader culture of care and mindfulness. Otherwise, it is more like bailing water out of a lifeboat. The rest of the book is dedicated to exploring how we can approach our leadership and classroom practice in a mindful way. Nonetheless, you are also responsible for your own health. It depends on others but starts with you – another paradox.

# Holding Yourself

If or when things get difficult, it can help to have some practices to 'hold yourself'. The intention of the introception practice and the attachment questions in Chapter 2 is to support you to develop your knowledge of yourself, both mind and body, particularly what stresses you and how and why you might respond in certain ways. This final practice builds on these and aims to allow you to step into a more authentic form of leadership that is secure and open to others.

It is a practice that can be done initially very intentionally as a form of psychic protection when you are not feeling strong. Over time it can become a habit, both a more natural or integrated way of being and a resource to draw on in times of stress. It requires taking only a few seconds before you enter the meeting, classroom or assembly to prepare yourself, much like an actor would prepare for going onstage. This approach has really helped me before difficult conversations or interviews. Think of it as the last bit of planning; you are, after all, the most valuable lesson resource. In Chapter 9 I will suggest how this might fit in amongst a routine for the students. It can also be done in moments of difficulty. If you find yourself having a stress response (for example, sweating, palpitations, quickened breathing or tensing muscles) or if you find yourself dis-associating from your body, either you can nip to the loo or do a more discreet version of the practice in the room. It is as follows:

## 'Holding Yourself' Practice

**Acknowledge:** Do a quick body scan. Where are you holding tension? How are you feeling? Notice non-judgementally any emotions that arise.

**Pause:** Breathe and be with what arises for a moment.

**Release:** In whichever way feels good for you, you could try a shakedown, starting with your arms then your legs and progressing to shaking your whole body. Or you could do some strong fire breathing (where you emphasise a fast exhale), or you might feel release by rolling your shoulders or rotating your neck. Yawning, sighing, laughing or even silently screaming can effectively release emotions stored in the body too.

**Centre:** Feel your feet on the floor. Notice your spine from your sacrum to the cranial bones at the back of your neck. Have your hands by your side, palms open. Be still and notice where your breath is coming from. Breathe into your belly and lengthen your exhalation. Look around you be in the now. Smile and enjoy it (you really do have the best job in the world). Then begin.

## Summary

- To have **good mental health** requires a '**balanced** diet' of activities **and modes of being**.

- **Focus** time, time to closely **pay attention** and learn new things, is important.

- But so are **play** time, **connecting** time (both with other people and with nature), making time for being **physically active**, **taking time** in (to reflect and be in your body), **non-goal-directed** downtime and **sleep** time.

- This requires a **shift in our mindset** because the temptation in the profession is to be 'on' all time.

● We must prioritise these things because they matter *and* because they will enable us **to lead in a more strategic and emotionally healthy way**.

## Notes

1 More information about this is available at www.forestryengland.uk/blog/forest-bathing.
2 Information available here: www.adultdevelopmentstudy.org/grantandglueckstudy.

# SECTION TWO
# Leading School Culture

# 4 A Middle Way

This chapter will do the following:

- Explore the dualistic way of thinking that dominates education
- Suggest a middle way out of these binary perspectives that values love and knowledge, structures and relationships

## Integration

'The middle way' is the term that the Buddha used to describe the path of moderation. He taught that the road between extremes led to enlightenment. This concept is not unique to the Buddhist tradition. In philosophy, the Aristotelian notion of the golden mean suggests a similar path. More recently, Interpersonal Neurobiology has identified integration, finding a balance between chaos and rigidity as the key to good health.

This is both on a lifestyle level. Think of the healthy mind platter and a psychological and interpersonal level. Interpersonal integration occurs where there is secure attachment – that is, where one is able to join with another whilst maintaining a differentiated identity. This is the hallmark of healthy parenting and is necessary for healthy relationships and communities as it enables an individual to extend a hand to others in distress without being overwhelmed themselves.

Integration is not an abstract phenomenon; it can also be seen at neural level. It is visibly apparent in brain scans. Healthy brains show balance between the hemispheres whilst a striking a number of conditions in the DSM-IV (the 'bible' of psychiatric disorders), from autism to schizophrenia, demonstrate notably similar damage to the integrative fibres of the brain (Siegal, 2012, p. 124).

## Cartesian Dualism

So what does this have to do with school leadership? Colleagues that have been in the game a while complain of seeing the pendulum swing back and forth between

DOI: 10.4324/9781003198482-7

binary positions: knowledge or skills, curriculum or pedagogy, zero-tolerance discipline or restorative justice. With each revolution, the proverbial baby seems to get thrown out with the bathwater. What is more, people seem to feel pressured to pick a side. No more so than on Twitter, though this plays out on the ground in schools too. It can feel so personal: either you are for the latest change, or you are dinosaur who (worst of all) does not care about the kids. However, the reality is far messier and more nuanced than this.

Palmer (2017) considers the broader epistemological shifts that have influenced this dualistic way of thinking. He suggests that the objectivism of the Enlightenment project – not to be confused with the Buddhist one – was an important reaction to the reckless subjectivity of the so-called 'dark ages'. He argues that victims of the black death would have benefited from the objective knowledge that their suffering was caused by fleas on infected rats and not a punishment from God (*ibid.* 53–54). However, this project, which intended to put truth on firmer ground, became enthralled by looking at things in an atomistic and external way at the expense of subjective ways of knowing.

Binary thinking, which casts mind against body and reason against emotion, is at the heart of this project. Descartes infamous statement 'I think therefore I am' sums it up. In the reason-driven epoch of the Enlightenment, the mind was valued most highly. In the Romantic period that followed, it was emotions, feelings and matters of the flesh. However, the same logic prevailed – that is, the notion that the mind and body are separate, that reason is independent of emotions and that we must reject one way of knowing to accept another.

Palmer makes the case that at times in modern history, rampant objectivism has conspired with other forces to deliver people into the clutches of totalitarianism. This has led to both a distrust of other more subjective ways of knowing and a fear of how that expertise might be manipulated (*ibid.*). This feels visibly clear in a post-truth, anti-vax world, where people have apparently 'had enough of experts' (Gove, 2016) and whoever shouts the loudest seems to have a claim on truth. We are affected by this hyper-rationalism and distrust at a school level too. We have become enthralled by externals – levels and league tables – yet relational trust is at an all-time low and parent and student complaints are at an all-time high.

This schism is evident in the therapeutic world as well as education. Empiricist approaches such as behavioural psychology and Cognitive Science are polarised against psychotherapy, psychoanalysis, and Eastern traditions such as mindfulness that deal with the more ineffable domains of the unconscious, intuition or spirit. However, newer scientific fields such as Interpersonal Neurobiology are bringing together many of these findings and highlighting the interconnectedness of the mind, body and relationships.

There is a role for empiricist and subjective ways of knowing in our work as school leaders. Large-scale studies or randomised control trials have an important role to play in ensuring equity in education. Organisations such as Research Ed and the Education Endowment Fund have been crucial in guiding the profession to use its finite resources in effective ways. However, none of this needs to come at the expense of individual relationships, feelings or listening and noticing what is happening on the ground.

## A Middle Way

With the notion of the Buddha's middle way in mind, I suggest we do not have to pick a side. Whilst I am not the first to try to find to try and find a middle way between 'traditional' and 'progressive' approaches, there are many that believe them to be at cross purposes in regard to the entire point of education. I suggest, however that different perspectives can enrich rather than cancel each other out. In positions that are often purported to be antithetical, there is plenty of common ground, and where there is difference, engaging with other points of view provides a helpful critique that enables us to see things more holistically.

This principle can be applied to the entirety of the educational endeavour. Palmer argues that when we reduce teaching to intellect, the form and concepts of how we know and learn it becomes an abstraction, but equally, if we reduce it to emotions – how we and our students feel – it becomes narcissistic. Education is both these things, and they depend on each other for their wholeness. As we saw in Chapter 2, on a neural level, our emotions cannot be disentangled from cognition. When we stop considering issues in an atomised way and move instead into a space of nuance, we can see the absurdity of many of the binaries we work with in education.

How can I be either for discipline or relationships when they are fundamentally interconnected? Healthy relationships require both connection and boundaries. Teachers' and students' needs are not separate but bound together. What binds them are the subjects we teach. We need to prioritise developing knowledge – in many different forms – but this must be held in a framework of values, love and safety. There are ways of getting things done and holding people to account that do not need to instil fear. To borrow a term from Mary Myatt (2016), we can provide 'high challenge' whilst being 'low threat'. In fact, to not do both does a disservice to everyone as our sense of well-being is deeply connected to our capacity to do a good job.

## Parenting

The inclination towards binary thinking influences parenting too. In fact, it is helpful to consider parenting trends because as Riley suggests, we might substitute the word 'parent' for 'teacher' and use the lens of attachment theory to understand what is needed to enable students to feel secure in the classroom (Riley, 2011, p. 651).

In her book *Hate Me Now, Thank Me Later*, Dr Robin Burman suggests that, as a culture, we have lost our way in terms of parenting. She argues, 'Somehow children went from being seen and not heard to being the center of the universe' and that by constantly trying to please our children, we have in fact done the opposite (2014, p. 2). She maintains that 'this pendulum swing has created a whole new breed of entitled, fragile kids' (*ibid.*). Burman attributes this shift to our fast-paced culture in which parents have lost their own perspective, equilibrium and internal peace. She suggests that they cannot offer something to their children that they do not themselves have.

Burman asks, 'Isn't there a graceful place in the middle of these parenting extremes? A hybrid approach in which we thoughtfully reflect upon what we should keep from our parents' methods, what we can learn from recent parenting trends, and what no longer serves us?' (*ibid.*, p. 3). The same can be asked of schools.

## Rules vs Relationships

Too often, discussions about school culture are polarised between those who prioritise relationship building and those who prefer establishing rules and routines. In the depths of the Twittersphere, terms like 'warm strict', an approach that recognises that the two are integral to one and other, have to be put in a box — 'right' or 'left', 'trad' or 'prog'. Dog whistles such as 'zero tolerance' or 'flattening the grass' are used to denigrate approaches seen to put outcomes before the needs of the whole child. They are mis-characterisations that seem to be perpetuated by some newspapers and those on Twitter with some book or consultancy to peddle — one that bears extraordinarily little resemblance to the warm and child-centred cultures I have witnessed first-hand in schools that take these approaches.

In this polarised environment, 'progressive' approaches are equally mis-characterised. Trauma-informed practices which exalt educators to become acquainted with many of the adverse childhood experiences (ACEs) that sit behind challenging behaviours and restorative-justice approaches that remind us of the role of repair and relationship in improving behaviour are accused of teacher blaming and the bigotry of low expectations.

That is not to say that there is not a danger if the pendulum swings too far. Restorative approaches have been criticised by a recent NASUWT study (2021) for putting the learning and welfare of students and teachers at risk by undermining consistency and shifting the burden of responsibility for behaviour onto classroom teachers. However, it seems likely that much of these issues are due to failures in school culture and implementation, perhaps a result of external pressures and not problematic ideas alone. There is a real difference between supporting adults to understand and take responsibility for the 'weather' they make in the classroom and restorative approaches that seek to blame teachers. Equally, in a culture of high expectations and adult authority, a well-handled restorative meeting ensures that children take responsibility for their own actions.

What is more, schools with more authoritarian, sanction-based systems can suffer from poor or unconscious implementation. They can slip into rigidity and perpetuate inequalities or serve the needs of the teacher at the expense of the needs of the child. Michael Young suggests that there is a fear on the left that that in turning away from child-centred approaches, we would be going back to the Gradgrind ethos of the Victorian era (2018). However, there is a path between rigid authoritarianism and boundary-less chaos, that 'graceful place' that Berman points to.

## Safety

Exploring the theme of felt security brings both perspectives together. I have had the privilege of working with several leaders who have rejected such binary stances. They might not share ideology or approach, but what they have in common is that their schools feel safe. They create a culture of co-regulation in which staff and students alike feel safe and secure enough to explore, try things out and learn. This requires teacher-leaders to have both attunement to people's needs *and* boundaries, like good parents do. That is the discernment to know when to cushion a child and when to 'empathetically let them fail'. This, in Siegal's terms, is how we find good health or integration.

Oli Knight wrote a beautiful blog post entitled 'Hate Me Now, Thank Me Later' (2018), based on Burman's (2014) book. In it, he espouses the role of rules and consequences alongside love and relationship building. In his school, kindness, respect, high expectations and boundaries are maintained through clear routines. By making the environment predictable and reducing the amount of unnecessary thinking (or cognitive load), these routines support children to feel safe and achieve success.

In his 2020 book, *Running the Room*, Tom Bennett argues that adult authority is key to establishing schools as safe spaces. In the wake of *Everyone's Invited* and the 2021 Ofsted report[1] into sexual violence in schools, the need to ensure our schools are safe for all has never been more pressing. The approach that Bennett – the so-called government 'behaviour tsar' – puts forward is often pitted against attachment-aware or trauma-informed practice. However, in my experience, it is often young people who have experienced multiple adverse childhood experiences (ACEs) who most need to feel the containment of clear and warmly held boundaries. Having worked as the SENDCo in a school dubbed 'zero tolerance', I can vouch that the predictability and security of all the adults consistently upholding high expectations creates a real felt sense of security.

As we have explored, recent theorising on attachment points to neuroplasticity, the ability of the brain to be 'rewired' as a result of a 'corrective emotional experience' of felt security (Doidge, 2007; Mate, 2003). It is an optimistic picture for young people who have experienced trauma, as there is potential to establish new neural pathways through relationships with consistent, emotionally attuned adults with good boundaries. If we can make schools secure bases, then over time we can reduce the felt experience of threat and therefore facilitate more positive relationships, reduce challenging behaviours and enable curiosity. Attachment theory teaches us that safety must precede curiosity. Therefore, this sense of safety is also prerequisite for meaningful learning.

When we feel we will not be judged, we can be open to others and try things out. A safe environment is therefore an environment where academic success can flourish. Stephen Lane describes this interplay between the academic and the pastoral, suggesting that we need to ensure that our provision is 'focused on ensuring that students feel safe and happy in school, so that they can attain, and that they attain so that they can feel safe and happy' (2020, p. 88), what he describes as 'the yin and yang of schooling' (*ibid.*).

This need for safety applies to students, teachers and leaders. We all need to feel safe and supported to flourish. It is our job as leaders to create the conditions that enable this, to create this secure base. Then everyone else can focus on the core work, making great learning happen.

## Subject Centred

If we acknowledge the alchemy that exists in the relationship between teacher and student, and the great things that are our subjects, we can traverse tired progressive (student centred) or traditional (teacher led) lesson debates. It is not that one is more important than the other but that the whole is greater than the sum of its parts. As Palmer suggests, we could prioritise making our schools subject centred (Palmer, 2017) – that is, places where teachers and students collaborate around great things, the artifacts of our curriculum. Not only does focusing on this circumvent an endless debate, but it also removes the ego from the classroom. It makes it all about the work.

Paradoxically perhaps, to do this requires also attending to relationships. For relationships to appear not to matter, they must really matter. Everyone has to feel valued so they know that nothing is personal. To achieve this requires positive, respectful relationships *and* respect of expertise without professing to know it all because the knowledge to be acquired is always endless.

## Cognitive Load Theory

Cognitive load theory (CLT) is an approach which draws on Cognitive Sciences' understanding of how we think, learn and solve problems. Perhaps due to its behaviourist origins, CLT has come to be associated with traditionalism in education and therefore may not be an obvious bedfellow of mindfulness. However, I suggest that the overlap is profound.

CLT posits that humans draw on three elements to learn: the environment, our working memory and our long-term memory (Lovell, 2020). Whereas the capacity of the environment and long-term memory are unlimited, working memory is restricted to between four and seven 'elements' of information (*ibid.*). This is what is called the cognitive load. That means there is only so much information we can hold in our head or tasks we can juggle at one time.

The implications of this finding for our classrooms and our leadership practices are significant. We must be strategic about what we choose to do as we cannot do everything. Prioritising reducing the strain on our working memory and moving things into long-term memory so that they are habitual become the goals of a CLT-informed leadership. We need to make sure we routinely do what we know works. This is as relevant to teachers' practice as it is to students.

Both mindfulness and Cognitive Science call for us to strip back the distractions and be intentional about where we put our focus. When we are not overwhelmed, we feel safe and can be successful. This applies as much to adults as it does young people and, of course, starts with ourselves. From our own place of clarity, we can be deliberate about where our students put their attention.

## High Challenge, Low Threat

When we make people feel safe and like they have purpose, we find that they are usually responsive to feedback and open to change. Making people feel this has in part to do with our own state of regulation, our regard for our teams and the quality of our relationships. However, it is also related to our expertise and how easily we provide clear frameworks for improvement that do not overwhelm our colleagues.

This requires us as leaders to know our subjects and to have forms of accountability that are meaningful and proportionate. When we are ill informed and insecure, it is easy to lose sight of what we are assessing or let the metric become the target. We reduce our lesson observations to a checklist, for example, rather than using it as a jumping-off point for a conversation about what makes great teaching. Some ways of holding people to account which are streamlined, effective and humane will be explored further in the next chapter.

Now, whilst I am arguing for a low-threat approach, that is not to suggest that there are not times when we might not need to hold a firmer position. Good leaders, like parents, hold boundaries. Sometimes mutations occur or things are really not good enough, and so some rebalancing needs to happen. However, most often it does not need to get to that point. What is key is that we do not operate from the default position of aiming to move people on or use the capabilities' process as a tool to whip people into shape.

## Love and Knowledge

In her excellent talk for *Research Ed*, 'Love and Knowledge in Leadership', Carly Waterman (2020), much like Palmer, locates the roots of the tired dichotomies between knowledge or values and 'trad' and 'prog' in the Cartesian distinction between emotions and reason. Of course, as we saw in Chapter 2, this no longer reflects the scientific understanding, yet education has continued to perpetuate this way of thinking. As Waterman suggests, in this context, certainties become cemented, and 'if you sit on the fence [you are] seen as weak and having no position'. Nonetheless, she says that she takes a middle way, what she terms 'respectful scepticism'. 'Have an opinion and then change your mind . . . it's okay. It's all learning', she suggests.

She draws on Matthew Evans' book *Leaders with Substance* (2020a), in which he argues that we have become focused on leadership as an abstract set of skills, values or heroic attributes at the expense of a specialist knowledge about the substance of our roles. They argue that this 'motivational quote' form of leadership has left our schools feeling the opposite of being well led. Waterman, however, brilliantly articulates how values-driven leadership, though difficult to define, is not incompatible with approaches to leadership that focus on developing domain-specific knowledge. The problem, she suggests, has been that a reductionist, pop-psychology approach has defined leadership as a set of personality traits or competencies to be ticked off, not the notion of values or, as she puts it, love. Waterman argues that knowledge is needed to build relational trust but references Steve Munby, who cautions that, unless we attend to the love side of leadership, we may not be successful in taking people with us towards our aim (Munby, 2020, p. 8). In doing this, though, she draws our attention to another paradox. Making the right decisions supported by knowledge is how you attract discretionary effort. If you lead with love, you want to lead with knowledge, and you get love by making good decisions. One begets the other.

She argues that domain-specific leadership elevates educational expertise and allows the exercise of values with fidelity, citing an example of a head teacher friend to explain how. In this example, a colleague with an ill child comes to the head, who tells her instantly, 'Take all the time you need. We'll pay.' Despite her values telling her this is the right thing to do, without the prerequisite knowledge of HR and the statutory and school-based procedures that influence this, there are potentially huge implications of making such promises. In this case, these constraints meant that the head let her colleague down. Waterman points out that you are not really a values-based leader if you make empty promises (*ibid.*).

This elevation of expertise does not mean we have to know everything or get it right all the time. We will always be greater than the sum of our parts. Waterman draws on John Tomsett's theme in his blog series that begins with 'This much I know' to emphasise that a leader is always learning. She suggests that in the previous example, a more authentic response would have been to say to the colleague, 'I want to be able to say 'Take all the time you need', but I need to check what the constraints are and make sure I give you an informed answer.' This not only recognises the importance of knowledge and humility in maintaining good relationships but speaks to the nuance of our roles as leaders at the interface of the professional and the personal.

Whilst there is a risk that I, too, am constructing another form of generic leadership with the term '*leading mindfully*', I hope it is clear that doing so also requires a solid foundation of knowledge. However, I would seek to broaden our definition of 'knowledge' to include relational knowledge, Interpersonal Neurobiology and self-knowledge alongside the more obvious domain-specific leadership. If we can model this humility and hunger for expertise, then we have taken the first steps to building a culture in which both learning and well-being are truly prioritised. The next chapter will explore how we might develop this further.

## Summary

- A **dualism** in Western thinking has led to an assumption that **reason** is **separate** from **emotion** and the **mind** is **separate** from the **body**.

- This plays out in the **education** discourse, which pits **traditional** values **against progressive** ones, **knowledge** against **skills** and **systems** against **relationships**

- These binary assumptions do not reflect the **reality on the ground** in schools, which is far **messier** and more **nuanced**.

- I make the case for a **middle way** that provides **accountability without fear** and acknowledges that **routines** *and* **relationships** *and* **love** *and* **knowledge** are **integral** to one and other.

## Note

1 www.everyonesinvited.uk/

# 5 A Safe Base

This chapter will do the following:

- Outline the role that trust plays in establishing a healthy culture and consider how we might generate it

- Understand some of the ways that we send 'hidden' messages through our leadership

- Explore how we can make our communication contingent with what we want to convey

When we become more mindful of what makes us feel safe and well – think back to the healthy mind platter explored in Chapter 3 – we can create more balance for ourselves. Once we do so, we are then able to do the same for our staff, who in turn can be more responsive and mindful leaders for the children we teach. I would argue this is our most important role as leaders.

Becoming secure in ourselves is just the first step. This chapter will explore the processes that mindful leaders might undertake to establish this as the cultural norm so that school can become a safe base for all to attach to.

To establish a culture where everyone feels a felt sense of security requires having clear, kind and well-communicated boundaries that are consistently held by all the adults in the building. In making responses predictable and aligned, we ensure that everyone knows what to expect. This is as important for adults as it is for children.

This kind of culture is not built overnight. Much of its success rests on the less glamorous work of attention to detail, implementation and maintenance. What is more, there is no dichotomy between *what* you do and *how* you do it – the middle way again. We must attend to how priorities are communicated and how boundaries are held – that is, how they make people *feel* – as well as ensuring we are introducing effective and evidence-based policies. So let us explore the active ingredients that make up such a culture.

DOI: 10.4324/9781003198482-8

# Trust

There is a strong correlation between trust and positive student outcomes, even once other variables are controlled for. Bryk and Schneider's (2002) study *'Trust in Schools: A Core Resource for Improvement'* demonstrated that relational trust has the power to offset several external factors that are usually determinants in poor student achievement. However, as Myatt argues, trust is a much-abused term (2020). There is often an expectation that it will be present, but rarely is the hard work done to earn it. She suggests that successful leaders realise that to begin with, there is no point complaining that it is not there. Creating trust is a top-down process and so it must start with the leaders (*ibid.*). Applying attachment theory to school leadership, Riley uses the metaphor of a river delta, suggesting that 'security flows like water from principal and leadership team as parent surrogate'. If the leadership dries up, then the delta (classroom and peer-to-peer relationships) suffer first (Riley, 2011, p. 93).

We cannot pay lip service to trust. This is the reason the work in Section One is so important. You must be clear and comfortable in yourself so you can be consistent and congruent with others. To truly trust those that you lead requires being secure in yourself. This is because to trust is to make yourself vulnerable. You open yourself up to the possibility that you or others may get it wrong. This is particularly hard as school leaders because, although we have grand titles, we are not really at the top at all. We are part of a complex web of accountability in a system that does not really trust *us* and where – particularly in recent times – the rules are always changing. Nonetheless, it is our job as leaders to resist this, to open that metaphorical umbrella and protect our staff and our children.

I think it is important to note that this does not mean I am advocating a free-for-all. There may be good reason not to trust a particular member of staff or student in certain situations. However, if you want to create an environment where learning flourishes, being untrusting should never be the default. We come back to the notion of the middle way again. Trust needs to be held within a framework of knowledge, high expectations and accountability, and you need to surround yourself with the right people. Communicate your expectations well and frequently, then let your team do the jobs you have employed them to do.

Nowhere is the lack of trust in our system exposed more starkly than in relation to subject specialisms. For too long, subjects have been shoehorned into generic pedagogies due to a lack of expertise at a leadership level and accountability pressures. In my own senior leadership experience, I have line-managed English, MFL and performing arts despite extraordinarily little teaching experience in these subjects, let alone experience of university-level scholarship. Christine Counsell (2018) has done crucial work in getting us to think about how we might develop a senior-curriculum leadership that respects the expertise of subject specialists, but more on this later. What is important is that we generate credibility. This comes from reflecting, listening, walking the talk and developing our domain-specific knowledge as leaders.

## Hidden Curriculum

In his excellent book on pastoral leadership in which he sets out his own middle way, Stephen Lane proposes the concept of the hidden curriculum (Lane, 2020, p. 57). He introduces this in relation to behavioural expectations, exploring the congruency between the messages given in public and the ones enacted in day-to-day practice. Trust can easily be undermined by incongruency in messaging. This is as much about what we do as what we say and as much what we do not do as what we do. If our body language does not match the words that we are delivering or if there are other competing initiatives, we can easily undermine our own message. For example, if staff are told that subject knowledge is valued but there is no CPD time set aside for it, or they are instructed to have restorative conversations with students who are given warnings at the end of every lesson but also that they must not be late for lunch duty.

Lane argues that we must think carefully about the messages given to students so that they are considered and cohesive. This notion can also be applied to the messages we give to staff. We do not all need to become advertising gurus, but part of leading mindfully is becoming clear on your vision and considering the messages that you might be unintentionally sending out. Communication is an important element of this.

## Mindful Communication

Mindful communication has two elements: it is streamlined, avoiding unnecessary distractions to focus on a core message, and it is human. How often do we hide behind email when we could have a conversation? The words we say and the effort we make matters. This is magnified when we are in leadership. A throwaway comment can have all sorts of implications, particularly in low-trust environments. Mindful leaders are attuned to this. They know that many problems can be solved and that people are much more inclined to put in discretional effort when they feel valued. Taking the time to talk to someone makes them feel valued.

Yet a mindful leader is economical with their frequency of communication and condenses things down to one or two simple messages where possible. Our use of email exploded in lockdown, and if we are not careful, it can easily overwhelm our staff and distract from their core work. A daily and weekly bulletin that funnels all communication through a single point of access ensures clarity of message, avoids duplication of work and prevents email overload. With the bulletin, the expectation is that staff read one email (properly) before the start of the working day. To make this happen requires a certain amount of forethought on the part of the leadership. They will not send emails at 10:00 p.m. (schedule send or no schedule send) not only because they are respectful of their team's time but also because they do not need to, as things are planned well in advance.

## Time

How often do we review policies and tell our team to stop doing things that are no longer relevant or not supported by evidence? Recent Teacher Tapp findings suggest this is rarely done.

When we introduce a new initiative, we need to consider the opportunity costs. What else could teachers be doing in this time and what will be taken away. As Paul Dix says, overworked teachers have initiative overload. They look at any request 'through a very sharp lens' (2017, p. 4). If they do not think they will still be asked to do something in six months, those colleagues that are more avoidant will not engage with it. Perhaps they will 'nod in the right places, fill in the paperwork' (*ibid.*) and carry on as usual. Those that tend to be more anxious might waste time stressing over the details of something that will be got rid of with the next cycle. However, if leaders can build the trust and belief that the change will truly make a difference, then everyone will adapt and buy in.

There is no stronger signal of what you value than how you spend your time. Time is limited, and we do not want our teachers (or students, for that matter, though it is usually less of an issue) working all hours of the day. If they do, they will be burnt out and be of no good to anyone.

How we use our own time and how we are seen to value the time of others conveys messages – that hidden curriculum again. If you are always rescheduling or never where you say you will be when your colleagues come to find you, do not be surprised if they don't feel valued by you.

A mindful approach to time management requires not overcommitting yourself. Decide on a few things that matter and do them well. This enables you to keep your promises. Mary Myatt says, 'When we give ourselves permission to stop trying to do it all, to stop saying yes to everyone, we can make our highest contribution towards the things that really matter' (2016, p. 36). When we lose the ability to filter what is important and what is not, we get 'decision fatigue' (*ibid.*). By making wise investments of time and energy, we can operate at this highest point of contribution, focusing on what is essential (*ibid.*) and doing that really well. The next chapter will explore what these few things might be.

## Humility and Complexity

A relentless focus on reducing workload is core to leading mindfully. In his chapter in *Research Ed Guide to Leadership*, Matthew Evans suggests that the primary role of a leader is to navigate complexity and work to reduce it. He argues that ignorance of complexity has led to a 'creeping managerialism' (2020b, p. 229). Driven by a desire to be seen to 'take action', leaders often make things worse by seeking to control the situation or provide simplistic solutions (*ibid.*). He advises recognising the limits of the influence of our leadership. He suggests that we should not attempt to control our environment too much or be too certain of our impact on it. Instead, he suggests that our role is to 'reduce disorder through simplification, stability and less uncertainty'. This is a subtle but crucial distinction. He cites an example of a novel review of mistakes in Child Protection Services. Where previous enquiries had simply identified who was to blame and found ways of controlling people so that they would be less likely to make those mistakes again, this new approach explored the systemic circumstances that led to these mistakes in the first place. There is a paradox, what Evans' describes beautifully as an 'an endless, evolutionary waltz' (*ibid.*). When we truly understand the complexity of the challenges we face, we are forced to respect the limitations of our role but we are also able to see more clearly what can be done to change things. He suggests this should be working to simplify our messaging and the demands placed on our teachers.

## Story

As Riley says, human knowledge is storied (2011, p. 74). We use narrative to communicate and make sense of the world. Siegal describes how stories capture the imagination of the youth and enable young people to take on the wisdom of the older generation whilst shaping and taking ownership of their futures. Meanwhile, Porges says, 'In telling the story of our own past, we are not the child anymore. We are the adult' (Porges, 2017, p. 200).

Dixons Trinity Academy have mastered the art of simplifying a message. In the same *Research Ed Guide*, their principal and executive principal describe how they use story and imagery to convey ideas and create a sense of belonging (2020b). The extended metaphor of a mountain is used to describe a student's journey at the school. Mountain Rescue is a holistic pastoral department that technically incorporates SEND, safeguarding, behaviour, first aid/medical attention, home-school liaison and transition, but in essence, it is much simpler – it is a pastoral department that does not care for categorising. The mindset is anyone might need support at any point in their school 'climb', but that this does not limit or define them (Dempsey, 2020). They just do whatever any student needs them to do at the time.

## Doing a Few Things Well

Top leaders tap into this unifying and healing potential of stories. We all need to belong, but young people's brains are particularly wired for this connection. As Oli Knight is fond of saying, we need to make 'school more compelling than the street' (Knight cited in Whitworth, 2019). To do this effectively requires a CLT-informed approach. We must decide what to focus on (and what not to) and then overcommunicate that message. This is our job as leaders. As Sparks and Thompson put it, 'Leaders shape a school vision and set the purpose. One person cannot steer a ship, but they do have to narrate the story of a school in order for the staff to know which direction to take with their everyday decisions and choices.' As Myatt reminds us, this culture should be 'lived not laminated' (2007), built into the systems of the school but coming to life in daily interactions. At Dixon's Sparks and Thompson say, 'There should be no hollow note, every interaction every day with every pupil needs to be reinforcing' (2020, p. 115).

Crucially, though, they also highlight that 'waltz' that Evans' described, saying that there must 'remain the potential to dismantle, to reshape, to de-clutter and clear away'. Learning in this way is a team endeavour; they remind us, 'That means no ego. It also means strength – we will do whatever it takes (tear it all down and start again) but we will do it as a team. No individual needs to pull so hard all the time; no one needs to break' (*ibid.*).

## Learning Culture

To establish this ethos, where everyone comes together around a shared and effective message, requires building a thinking and learning culture. People must understand and buy into the vision; otherwise, they will need far too much cajoling for it to be efficient. As leaders we have to carve out time in our day, week and year for reflection and reading in order that we can be clear-headed enough to 'narrate this story' but also build a thinking and learning culture so that our teams are engaging with research themselves (Figure 5.1). If our teachers understand the ideas behind an approach, this can mitigate many of the lethal mutations of badly implemented policies. A mantra for leading mindfully might be 'We listen, we read, we reflect deeply, then we act.'

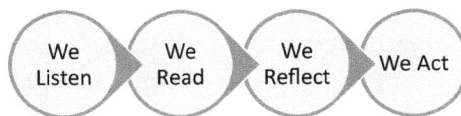

**Figure 5.1** Graphic illustrating the mantra for leading mindfully. That is, listening, reading, reflecting and then acting.

Having a school CPD library and setting aside time for reading and reflection is one way of doing this. Early in my career, I had the privilege of working with Laura Ellener, now head teacher at Chiswick School. One thing she did as lead for teaching and learning was to introduce a book club. This was amazing. As a beginner teacher, it allowed me to engage with the ideas that were shaping our policies in the school and to feel part of it, as well as reflecting on my own lessons and building a community of practice to do this with.

Building a learning culture involves modelling mistakes, accepting that we cannot do, know or be everything and having an openness to feedback. We teach students about the importance of having a growth mindset (Dweck, 2012). I have done more assemblies on Austin's butterfly (Berger, 2012) than I can count, yet we do not always apply the principles to ourselves. Again, Ellener was key in showing me this early on. Despite the gulf in our expertise, she invited my feedback on one of her own assemblies. Then not only did she take it on board, but she publicly celebrated what she had learnt from me. The effect of this on me and others was powerful. Happily, I can now publicly celebrate her in the interview below.

---

**Laura Ellener, Head Teacher at Chiswick School, Discusses Her Approach to Building a Learning Culture That Looks After Everyone's Well-being**

I have learnt the most from going into other people's schools. Recently, I've really liked what has been coming out of the Greenshaw Learning Trust. So I asked Joe Ambrose to come for six weeks and work with some of our leaders and talk about the way they did things. They have been exceptionally open and generous and let our staff go and look around their schools too. Sometimes you can get blinkered. It is important, however long you have been in your school, to keep outward looking, to see how others do things in different contexts to develop your thinking around what will make the student's and staff's experience the best it can be, whether that is in terms of outcomes or well-being. You also need to draw on the expertise in your own school, but you have to know at what point to look outside. That means knowing your staff, what skills they have and where you might need to go and get something that isn't yet there but could be with a nudge.

Reading is really important for building a thinking culture. However, having time to read can be difficult, so blogs can provide a helpful snapshot. The pandemic has also provided new opportunities for sharing. We are a standalone academy. Academies Enterprise Trust (AET) looped me in their network so that every week I got their head teachers' Covid-19 bulletin. This meant I didn't have to pore over all the updates. They were summarised, instead, by a central person.

There is a lot more sharing between trusts now, at least the outward-facing ones. I think there is a generation of school leaders who are more open and understand that sharing is something to be celebrated and that keeping everything to yourself is a strange way of operating as a school leader. The pandemic helped foster this sense of being all in it together.

I try to maintain this outwardness in my own leadership. Being a head teacher is so different from anything I had ever experienced. You have to make hundreds of decisions every day, and you have to make the right decisions because the buck stops with you. If you close in, then you are not going to make the right choices because you are only going to rely on your own experiences. For some decisions, you have to look outside and seek other expertise and opinion. Ultimately you have to make the final decision, but if you are closed, it can be dangerous. However, you also have to be able to make tough choices; it is equally dangerous when nobody makes them, but you have to remain open and willing to listen.

This is the most tiring thing about being a head and why having a good network is so important. In Hounslow we have a great network. Everyone is really willing to help and offer opinions.

As a head, you have to be prepared to not have an ego. When you get it wrong, you have to be able to say, 'Stop. Let's do something different.' I don't find it difficult to say 'I think I've got this wrong' or for someone to tell me that I have. Sometimes you say, 'I value your opinion, but we are going to do it this way.' I trust that I am making the right decision based on knowledge and integrity, but I also listen and change.

In the first three months of headship, I learnt a lot. I learnt you have to be who you are. You can't be someone else; that's exhausting. I've seen that others try to be the fierce, authoritarian know-it-all, and it's been very detrimental.

The time that you most have to not be yourself is at the beginning of new role. When you move, there is a guard that goes up because you don't know who you're working with or what their beliefs and knowledge are. You don't yet know whether they are on board with the direction you want to take the school in. This is sensible to have at first, but it passes with time as you get to know your colleagues and understand them. It is why you need a team where you can trust each other, that is open and doesn't blame each other.

I've led a few schools in crisis that are either in Special Measures or repeated RI and need to be 'got to good'. As a leader, you do have to be the captain of the ship. There is a time and place to say, 'This is what we are going to do and this is how.' This can be quite uncomfortable for everyone, especially if they've been part of that school for a while. It is easy to say 'We've done that before' or 'That won't work', but you push on because you know it will. It is not easy, but there are ways that it can be done.

However, you have to bring people with you. If you operate that way beyond the first six months, there is a problem. Things should have improved enough for everyone to think, 'This is a lot better that it was.' Someone said, 'Tighten to good, loosen to outstanding.' It's not for Ofsted, but that is a good way of looking at it. Once you are in a certain position, you can loosen a little, but you've got to keep pushing forward and being ambitious, just in a slightly different way. At that stage, it is about having a team that is bought into the vision, where everyone is moving in the same direction and really happy to be doing it.

You need to galvanise people and make them feel like they are a part of something special, something that is bigger than ourselves, which it is. We are building a kind of magic about where the school could go. People are generally really proud to be moving a school from a position of failure to somewhere where the children are thriving. But everybody does have to dig deep and heave.

Therefore, we have to make sensible choices about people's well-being. That means stripping back and making things really simple, no triple marking or anything like that. We talk about what we are doing and why. For example, we are looking after your well-being and removing four meetings from your calendar that we don't really need. We are going to have this one meeting, and it will be purposeful.

Well-being is not about giving people a cake on a Friday; it is about thinking about how you can, for example, sort out behaviour so it's not stressful for teachers to teach in the classroom. This requires listening to staff and checking the climate often, through surveys but also just talking to people and watching. You can tell a lot from looking at interactions and seeing how staff are behaving and reacting towards things.

What was really hard was the TAG process. It had to be done, and it was a huge, pressured amount of work for staff. We put in an extra INSET day. We told parents we wanted to do the process properly. We couldn't change the process, but by giving teachers some time to moderate well, we could alleviate a little of the stress. It is also just about being transparent about what we couldn't alleviate because it came from central government. Staff get really annoyed when they feel leaders are not being honest and open. Communication is really important. Through the pandemic, I sent out a Friday-afternoon bulletin telling everyone what was going on. This was something staff could read at their own leisure and meant there were no surprises. I have carried this on.

In terms of my own well-being. I'm a very resilient person. I am able to take a pragmatic view when things get very stressful. I think it is my makeup – my professional makeup, that is. In my life, I am quite a balanced person but when I went into teaching and leadership, friends thought it was hilarious because I also know how to switch off and have fun. Though I do far less of that now. I also really love my job. I feel like I'm giving a service and that it has a purpose. That is to support young people to have really good lives when they leave school because they have good qualifications, and they are good people. This sustains me.

## Walking the Talk

Paul Dix points out that nothing destroys an initiative more quickly than it not being seen to be taken seriously by the leadership. He describes an example of working with a school to introduce a behaviour approach, only to see it ruined overnight when rumours spread of SLT seeing an infringement and walking by instead of applying the agreed techniques (2017, p. 12).

As leaders we are always on show, so we must practice what we preach. If we have unworkable policies, we might exhaust ourselves doing so. Therefore, we must really know what we are talking about before we introduce a policy. We cannot just pull something off The Key or Twitter and expect it to work. It is that interplay of love and knowledge again. What is more, if a policy we have introduced is not realistic for or working in our context, we must respond to that rather than burying our heads in the sand.

One way to avoid this is to ensure you have really understood what the impact of a new policy or initiative will look like on the ground for a teacher with a five-period day or a pastoral leader who might be pulled into an urgent safeguarding meeting at any moment.

In his brilliant blog series from 2018, Ben Newmark (2021) explores why so many school behaviour strategies fail. He suggests that some of it is in the failure to think things through and involve the stakeholders that will implement it. Therefore, when a colleague grouches, 'How am I going to have time to hold twelve behaviour conferences in one day when I teach all day and have after-school intervention?' this should not be dismissed as being work shy or difficult. Our systems must be simple enough to administer in a reasonable working day, and teachers need to have the rationale behind decisions explained in order for them to buy into them.

With a reduced timetable and status of being on the SLT, it is easy to forget how difficult year 9 can be on period five on a Friday. If we do not think through the detail and make the decisions about what to prioritise then our staff end up doing it. This both makes them vulnerable and leads to inconsistency. We need to come towards our teachers with the assumption that they, like all of us, want to do the best for the kids. We need to continually be mindful of our team's workload and well-being if there are barriers to implementing our initiatives, we need to reflect on what conditions we as leaders need to change to ensure that these barriers no longer exist. If we add something, we must ask ourselves what we are taking away.

## Listening

Now we do not have to have all the knowledge of what will work ourselves. One way to really understand what is realistic is to ask the people on the ground doing the work already. Often, though not always, if given a platform, they have valuable insights into how their jobs can be improved. We can draw on the support of others, and in doing so, not only do we gain a richer understanding of the potential pitfalls and successes of a plan, but we also bring others alongside us. Mary Myatt suggests pausing to reflect in this way is one of the most powerful ways in which trust is embedded (2020). The rich and subjective knowledge of your staff body is a huge resource and pays dividends in many ways. She tells us 'One of our greatest needs in life is to have our voices heard. It touches the deepest part of our being when we have the right to speak and be heard' (2016, p. 30). However, we listen not just to make others feel good but also because alternative perspectives are how we grow. Thoughtful leaders recognise this, and they make sure that there is time and space for this in the school calendar.

There are different ways of inviting others in. Gathering meaningful staff and student voices is important, and reflection tools like the 360 can support this. Yet the informal feedback that you gather from walking around and talking to people is priceless. However, if people are going to approach you, then you have to *be* approachable – that is open and seeming to have time.

Inviting others in helps us. We do not want a team of yes people. We want diversity in terms of knowledge, experience and perspective so we can have as broader a view as possible. Not only does gathering our colleagues' feedback provide greater understanding of the potential sticking points and workload implications of our policies. It also allows us to model leadership, both in terms of the fact that we seek feedback and the type of questions we ask. Mindful leaders might set the tone but they do not hog the strategic decision-making. This is because they know that by building opportunities for those they lead to think deeply about the nature of their role and see its successes that meaning is found. If we want to grow and retain brilliant leaders, we must ensure they have a sense of meaning and purpose and have the skill set to take on the role when they are ready. Furthermore, extending openness in this way builds relational trust. It is put 'in the bank', so to speak, for if difficult conversations need to happen. This is because when people feel they are valued and part of something, they are far happier to be held to account.

Listening does not always come naturally to us, and not all forms of it are equal. Often we are busy rehearsing our responses in our heads or planning the next question. To listen mindfully is to do so without prejudging, with open ears and open hearts. This means being really present, making eye contact and fighting the impulse to interject or fill silences.

## Research

Engaging with research is also key. Sometimes our colleagues are just too close or bogged down with the minutiae to see the big picture. One of the tenets of mindfulness is pausing to reflect and engaging with things as they are. An important element of leadership is looking at the evidence, not just how we would like things to be. Chapter 6 will suggest what some research-informed priorities of strategic and streamlined leadership might be.

However, ultimately it is not either people or policy but both. For a policy to be implemented well, it has to be based on solid (evidenced based) foundations and you have to bring people with you. It must respond to the specific context, *and* it has to be based on what the evidence says will be effective. Once we have introduced it, the effort does not stop; we must work continually to maintain it well.

## The Power of Practise

When we are able to openly celebrate our mistakes, we are able to play and be creative in our practice. The role of 'practise' as a verb is key here. Much like with mindfulness mediation, we must accept that there is no perfect state to be achieved, just constant evolution. But this evolution over time can lead to incredible results. As Aristotle famously said, 'We are what we repeatedly do, excellence therefore is a habit'.

One thing that many high-performing schools have in common is that they often place an emphasis on role-playing teaching techniques prior to using them in the classroom. At Dixons, for example, they do this every morning. At Reach Academy in Feltham, school ends early on a Wednesday to allow teachers CPD time to practise and embed techniques. Chapter 9 features an interview with Reach's Assistant Headteacher, Claire Couves, which will explore one such technique in more detail. As Claire is fond of saying, we practise not because we cannot do the technique but so we can do it without thinking. Then it can become part of our habitual practice.

Not only does role-play in this way allow teachers to develop good habits, but it also support them to be playful, creative and connected, what you need in a good team. Remember Porges' discussion of the social engagement system and the role of reciprocal play in allowing new neural patterns to fire up? Playing in this way allows us to loosen our ego just a little.

Again, this needs to be led from the top. If the leadership are not seen to get involved, it will not work, but if you are seen to be rolling you sleeves up, having a laugh and making yourself a little vulnerable, it will do wonders for your school culture. As Mary Myatt says, it 'takes the confidence of great leadership to be prepared to be exposed to this degree' (2016, p. 34). Mindful leaders do not set themselves up as being perfect because they know that perfection does not exist. In making themselves vulnerable in this way, mindful leaders create a safety net for others. They make it okay for their team to make mistakes because 'there are no recriminations, only discussion about what might be better' (*ibid.*). This is essential in the formation of trust, which is necessary for real learning to take place.

## High Challenge/Low threat Accountability

A learning culture cannot flourish where there is fear. This does not mean we cannot hold people to account. We just need to ensure that our systems for doing so respect the wholeness and integrity of that which we are monitoring and are low stakes enough so that no one feels they must perform for them. Then we have to actually use the data gathered for something meaningful, to improve teaching and learning, and staff need to know and feel the impact of this.

Drawing on Myatt's (2016) notion of 'high challenge, low threat', there are ways to regularly take the temperature of your school that are low stakes and supportive. The next chapter will explore what a mindful approach to CPD might be, but it is helpful to first return to the notion of school as a safe base – specifically Popper and Mayseless' (2003) conception of leaders as substitute parents, to consider the philosophy behind this. Much like healthy child development, effective professional development needs to happen within a secure-attachment relationship. There is a delicate dance between supporting someone and holding them to account and empathetically failing them in a way that enables growth. Our monitoring and feedback must be held in a framework of clear and possible expectations and unconditional positive regard. Some colleagues do not make it easy, but we must be genuinely committed to growing people, not caching them out.

To do this requires us to be mindful about how and what data we gather on our teams, ensuring that everything we do is focused on making our teachers and support teams better. This principle extends to all forms of evaluation, not just lesson observations. That means no pointless audits, lengthy performance management or performative book scrutinies.

The answers to the question of how we can make our teams better comes from both internal and external sources, which is why engaging with the research, student work and the experiences of our colleagues and students is key in this process.

Everything should be about enabling deep learning to happen. In the next chapter, Corrine Flett explains the 'deep dive' approach they have been taking at her school. This is about as far from a quick win or checklist as you can get. It is an approach that takes time and is rich in subject knowledge and different forms of data. It seeks to get a holistic understanding of where things really are rather than encouraging showing off.

Instructional coaching is another way of making sustainable change to classroom practice over time. Explored further in the next chapter, it is both relational and practical. It thrives because of the low-stakes nature and the relationship built between coach and coachee. This makes it a safe-enough space for people to be open to feedback and try things out in their practice. However, this relationship is built because people feel the value of it. They can see lesson by lesson that their coach is making a difference to their practice.

## Difficult Conversations

If we have worked hard to build a culture of trust then we have something 'in the bank' when difficult conversations have to be had. When we do so, it is important is that we do not lose sight of anyone's humanity. No matter how frustrating a colleague is, we must never try to catch them out. This requires extending that unconditional positive regard that we so freely have for our students – that everyone can improve, that no one is a lost cause – to those we lead too.

We must be informed and in our own integrity to do this. As Waterman says, we must speak from a place of love and knowledge. We must know our stuff so we can lead in line with our values. Take time to prepare yourself for these conversations, emotionally and with the requisite knowledge. The 'Holding Yourself' practice at the end of chapter 3 can support with this.

Then really *be* in the room, keep your feet on the floor and make eye contact. This helps us to keep the sight of the human and say what needs to be said. People usually know what is really going on even if we do not say it, and our survival brain often jumps to the worst conclusions. Remember polyvagal theory: if we are not regulated and coherent, we 'leak', and people will come away from our office thinking 'They hate me', 'I am not good enough', 'They want me gone' or whatever their attachment story is, even if that is not what we actually say.

# Building a Secure Base Reflection Questions

Below are some questions designed to help you reflect on how much of a secure base you are providing through your leadership. They could be done individually in your journal or in discussion with colleagues.

- Do you really welcome feedback, or do you pay lip service to it? How do you know? What changes as a result of your listening?

- Do you find yourself overcommitting to things? Are your asks always coherent and realistic? What might the impact of this be for you and others?

- Do you follow through on all of your promises? Do you walk the walk? If you say something is not tolerated, do you stop and address it every time you see it?

- Can you say the same for all those you lead? How do you know?

- How do your accountability procedures make your staff feel? How do you know?

- Do you feel comfortable to make or share mistakes with your team? Is that ethos shared throughout the school? How do you know?

- Do you always approach difficult conversations from a place of integrity? If not, how might you change that?

## Summary

- Creating a culture of felt security in your school requires you to be a **secure adult**, to both be attuned to others' needs and hold and communicate clear boundaries.

- Building trust **comes from the top**, so it starts with you doing the work on yourself.

- As leaders we are always on show, and therefore, we must be **clear** and **congruent**; otherwise, we end up communicating **hidden messages**.

- What we devote **time** to and how committed we are to **listening** and **learning** signals our priorities and whether or not it is a safe environment for people to try things out.

# 6  Streamlined Schools

This chapter will do the following:

- Make the case for prioritising reflection as leaders
- Explore some of the priorities of a mindful leader: getting relationships and expectations right, investing in professional development, putting the curriculum at the heart of everything, attending to what creates a sense of belonging in the school and community

## Reflection

As senior leaders, we wear a variety of hats: chaperones, bouncers, detectives who review CCTV, invigilators who monitor exams, even lollipop people on crossings. All these roles are valuable, but what we are paid for is our strategic thinking and our ability to bring people with us. This can only come with some space. Taking time to slow down and reflect as a leader allows you to get clear on what matters. When we move fast, we do not always have the space to properly digest what the research tell us will have an impact or attend to how our school community feels. From a place of metaphorical stillness, you can more easily prioritise doing things in line with your values and the evidence, that middle path of love and knowledge.

One of these things is to listen. Often, we are told that strong leaders are decisive. However, there is a paradox at the heart of making space for others in this way. When we open ourselves up to doubt and diversity, it actually allows us to be firmer in our conclusions. This is because we are more informed and so can make decisions from a place of knowledge. We know that we are greater than the sum of our parts, so in this slowing down, we must also make time for listening. This process is iterative; it creates the space to continue to listen, reflect, simplify and improve.

Amongst the busyness and pressure of schools, it is easy to get tempted by quick fixes or to elevate the tools (the admin, the grades) over the core work. Reflection helps bring us back to what really matters and to define the long-term goals. When

DOI: 10.4324/9781003198482-9

were guided by love and knowledge, we do what is right for our communities, not what is simply going to get us a better Progress 8 score. That is not to say that data and reputation are not important, but they are not an end in themselves. Paperwork and data support us, but they are not our work. *That* is educating our children. Oli Knight takes the approach of mapping all areas of school leadership back from a five-year plan. Safe in the knowledge that you are on track but that you cannot do everything all at once, this allows you to have the breathing space to be creative in the moment and resist the temptation of quick fixes. Crucially, though, it is not the plan itself that matters but the careful thinking it enables and the ethos it lives and breathes.

This ethos will not develop without it being given space. It is helpful to consider how you build *time in* into your school culture. This starts with yourself. If you are constantly on duty and in meetings, you will have no time to reflect. If you are not reflective, it is not reasonable to expect anyone else to be. It flows from your leadership.

Reflection time must be done meaningfully or it will become a yawn-inducing exercise. Your team will know if you do not buy into it. So will the students. Some schools have reframed exclusion and detention as reflection time too. This has real potential, but for kids to buy into it, it has to be handled well, with a healthy dose of relationships in there too. Section Three will consider some ways to support reflection and reconciliation at a classroom level, but let us first consider the 'few things' a mindful school might do really well. Again you might like to do this individually or in your journal.

## Reflecting on Reflection

- How is teaching time balanced with time to observe, reflect and plan?

- Does your leadership team teach?

- Does this give them enough time for their other duties as well as keeping their 'finger on the pulse' in terms of classroom practice?

- Is reflection time built into the meeting and CPD schedules?

- Are there meaningful opportunities for students to reflect built into the lesson, the day and the year too?

- What mechanisms do you have for gathering and acting on meaningful feedback from staff, students and the wider community?

## Priorities

Everyone's contexts are different, but I have distilled some general themes from both the research and my own experience. Whole books have been written on what I am attempting to digest in a few paragraphs, so I would encourage you, dear reader, in the spirit of leading mindfully to engage with the research as well yourself, if you have not already.

First and foremost, we must get relationships and expectations right. Otherwise, behaviour will be out of control, the school will not be safe and nothing will really get done. Convey clear messages through simple and easy-to-use systems, and create as much certainty and predictability for both students and staff. Then have a relentless focus on teaching and curriculum. This is the core work that school leadership is there to facilitate. Streamline everything else that does not serve this as much as possible. Follow the research but not as a checklist. Instead really understand it so you can implement it well and avoid the lethal mutations that can so easily emerge when research becomes policy. Have a coherent and low-stakes approach to CPD that responds to the needs of your students and your staff. Provide plenty of time to read, reflect and practice. Then simplify and streamline.

In his excellent book *Slow Teaching*, Jamie Thom (2018) suggests developing an ethos of minimalism, first by decluttering the physical environment. This habit of prioritisation and frequent clearing can then be extended to everything we do. Given space, we can reflect on our policies and procedures and ask what works (both for our setting and according to the research) and what is absolutely necessary. It is amazing how much we find we can streamline. Marking? Focus on feedback. Written reports? Encourage teachers to call home as and when things arise. Displays? Blank walls can be very calming. Must-have displays? Invest in something permanent that will age well. Excessive resourcing? Prioritise developing strong curriculum resources that can be used year after year.

Mary Myatt reminds us that sometimes people need weaning off unhelpful teaching habits. Where teachers feel insecure, these habits can become a comfort blanket (Myatt, 2020). This can apply to leadership too. When our fear creeps in, it is tempting to retreat into our paperwork, but do careful minutes need to be taken for every meeting? It is the conversations and the actions agreed that matter. Do we need to oversee everyone's line management minutes, or can we trust our direct reports to do their jobs? What if we asked ourselves if we really needed to have that meeting at all? Could it be an email? Face-to-face connection matters, but so does people's time. A mindful leader has the discernment to know the difference. Freed from unnecessary bureaucracy, we are able to focus on the things that really make a difference: relationships and expectations, professional development and curriculum.

## Relationships and Expectations

When it comes to establishing behavioural expectations and building positive relationships, they are two sides of the same coin. Students need to feel they are held and respected, that the adults are in charge and that things are fair. To do this, expectations need to be crystal clear. Then everyone knows where they stand.

From a leadership point of view, this requires thinking through the details and responses to different scenarios. Crucially this requires thinking about what we will not do, where we draw our lines, where we take responsibility as adults and where we might put the onus on the children.

This concept is underpinned by high expectations. It is our students' right to have access to a safe and secure school, a curriculum that broadens their horizons and opportunities to learn how to be functioning members of a community. To get them there, the adults need to be relentlessly consistent and predictable.

Chapter 9 will explore how we might achieve this in the classroom. This is not easy to do, and whilst there are some tips and techniques to help hold yourself in this way, which I will explore more in Section Three, it ultimately requires the adults to be secure in themselves and in the expectations of the school. This is so that they function as a web, reinforcing the same clear expectations of the students.

To be effective, these expectations need to be held within a clear and supportive whole-school approach. Any behaviour system needs to be easy for the children to understand and follow and simple for the teachers to administer. Getting the operational side of things right here makes a huge difference. That means realistic expectations about what teachers are expected to follow up on, a sensible information management and centralised, same-day consequences (be that detention or something else).

This allows everyone to feel clear and supported. Young people need to know that the adults are in charge, that they do what they say they will and that they are all working together. Teachers need to *feel* that the leaders have their backs. Then they can hold boundaries with the pupils without it being personal. They can say, 'This is just how we do things here.' When this happens, the children know what to expect of all adults. This sense of trust can be transferred to other relationships, building their resilience and social skills.

This is easily undermined. For example, if a teacher has removed a child from their lesson and they are returned by a busy leader who has a meeting to get to and who has been assured by the child that they will behave now, this lack of solidarity, of batting the problem back to the teacher, does irreparable damage to the trust between teaching staff. This creates cracks that ultimately make the students feel less secure. Where there is even a hint of teachers being out on their own or that the systems or routines are too difficult to implement consistently, staff end up having to use their personalities or individual relationships to try and survive. At best this is inefficient, but at as seen in Chapter 2, we do not always go to the best places under stress. When behaviours are too much to cope with and the expectations are not clear, there are all sorts of inconsistencies in practice that emerge, including turning a blind eye, sarcasm and threats.

There must be clear consequences that are immediate and proportionate where expectations are not met. Kids do not do well with delayed gratification, particularly those who do not get consistency at home. Consequences must come with a narrative as to why, that separates the behaviour from the person and conveys how much you care about them, their teacher and their subject, what Paul Dix describes as 'deliberate botheredness' (2017, pp. 37–52). This does not mean you get in an endless back and forth. You are the adult and you do not need to justify yourself, but students do need to understand *why* particular behaviours are expected of them and crucially be taught what good behaviours look like.

A good behaviour system actively teaches and celebrates the behaviours that we want to see and provides plenty of positive praise for doing so. Furthermore, there must be opportunities for repair in any behaviour system.

Unlike Dix, I do not see an incompatibility between warmly held sanctions and a restorative-justice approach. My main disagreement with the latter is that it should not be the sole approach and that any restorative practice needs to take into consideration what is realistic for teachers. There are only so many restorative conversations you can have in one day or with one child before you are left feeling exhausted and undermined. My suggestion is use it where it is appropriate, but do not shy away from providing consequences either. As long as they are delivered with kindness and consistency, most children (including those with attachment needs) will get on board with the rules. Where there are consequences for mis-demeanours, they should be dealt with centrally by the leadership and pastoral teams. When teachers are not caught up with setting and chasing detentions, they can then get on with their primary job of teaching, and students will have a much more consistent experience.

Finally, it is important to remember that any behaviour system is a tool, not an end in itself. I am sure we have all been guilty of becoming too institutionalised by our behaviour procedures, but the children are perhaps the most susceptible to this. The kids need to be reminded of the *why* of the system if they get too wrapped up in the language of red cards, S3s or whatever incarnation your behaviour policy takes. The conversations around consequences are what matters. These build the intrinsic motivation to be kind to others and stay focused on learning.

None of this is self-evident. Leading behaviour requires clear decision-making and communication because every individual has a different threshold of accept-able behaviour. Mindful leaders are bothered enough to carefully think through the implications of their requests and brave enough to be clear about what they will and will not allow. This clarity is liberating for everyone. When leaders take responsibility and set the tone, it is not up to individual teachers to fight battles over equipment, uniform or language. They are held in a web of culture that says, 'This is how we do things here.'

Nonetheless, this is not a dictatorial approach or a faceless bureaucracy. Lead-ers have to attune to the needs of their teachers and students and be prepared to change course if something is not working without bending to the whims of every disgruntled student or parental complaint. It is a delicate dance. When implement-ing a behaviour policy, attending to how it makes people feel and how easy is it to make happen amongst the other things you are already asking of them matters. If people cannot or will not buy into it, it just will not work.

Changing student behaviour was key to many of the successful transformations we made at Phoenix Academy, which was at the time the most improved school in London. My former colleague Tom Phillips reflects on the impact of the work that we did and more recent challenges with implementing a warm/ strict approach to behaviour.

**Tom Phillips, Deputy Head Teacher, Reflects on his Approach to Leading Behaviour and Inclusion**

The first thing that we did to shift culture was to change the behaviour policy. Initially it was all about gaining compliance from the students, with the long-term aim of creating a culture of learning behaviours. Compliance happened quickly, in the first five or six weeks. The task of bringing *all* students on board with our full expectations took longer.

Before we arrived, the children ran the school. It was an unsafe environment, with reports of students regularly bringing weapons on site. In the previous year, one of the heads of year had been chased down corridor by a group of year 11s. What was really evident when I did a pre-visit was the way children spoke to staff with a real lack of respect. What was also clear was that they had not been taught how to speak to adults respectfully. There was also a near-miss incident with a pencil case that flew from an upstairs window into the playground.

We began by setting out very clear boundaries. The September INSET was extended to a full week of training to ensure we overcommunicated the new systems and expectations to staff. Then the student induction was used to communicate to the children, 'This is how it is going to be', and set out a framework of specific rules for them to follow, with clear consequences if they did not. We also taught an explicit curriculum of behaviour so that people knew exactly what was expected of them and why. We did this through our PSHE curriculum, assemblies and our reflection-room mentoring. We also bought into a mentoring programme and, in our second year, created our own alternative provision.

A large number of students pushed back against the rules in week one. They were not used to the expectations, nor did they expect us to last or follow through, having seen new leadership teams come and go. By week three, the number of students not meeting expectations had drastically reduced. Most of the students realised we were not going to let up. As the students got used to us and the higher levels of expectations, we saw the improvements in their leaning environment, and the number of incidents of negative behaviour reduced even further.

Unrelenting, absolute consistency was key. This meant that sometimes difficult but supportive conversations with any staff seen to be wavering on the rules had to be had. As soon as you let one person walk past in a hoodie, the students will think they can get away with it with some people, and that makes it harder for everyone. They are testing you. If they can, they will say, 'I walked past three members of staff, and no one else challenged me. Why are you?' We ensured that everyone saw it as their responsibility to challenge everything they saw and not just the job of the pastoral staff or SLT. Obviously, these teams were very supportive, but it was key to ensure the students knew they would be held accountable for any inappropriate behaviour by any member of staff.

It is not really about the hoodie, but holding the line is important. Otherwise, some young people will prod away at the rules to see what else they can get away with. What is in your policy has to be enacted, so you have to think carefully about your policies. Kids benefit from the boundaries and will see it as a weakness if you do not follow through on them.

We introduced a tiered behaviour system. Everything was an opportunity to learn but small mistakes require a different response to genuinely bad decisions. We were also very clear on what behaviours required a warning (to amend their behaviour) and what received an instant sanction. That way, everyone knew where they stood. It made it less personal. We used to say, 'Hate me now, thank me later' a lot. Our intention was to support students to develop a more resilient mindset, to understand that disappointment is a temporary obstacle. I often give students an example of my getting three motorbike fines in a week for riding my motorbike in the same bus lane. In that situation, I had genuinely not understood that I was not allowed to ride in a bus lane as I could not see the sign and didn't realise that different boroughs have different rules. So I wrote a polite letter explaining that I had made a mistake and asked if they could reduce the fine. They said no, I appealed and they still said no. In the end, I had to accept it and move on. In a school context, we teach the children to deal with things politely and accept it when they do not always go their way. Quite often they will receive a sanction that they did not believe was warranted, but we wanted to create a culture of responsibility for behaviours.

Rules and boundaries got us so far, but there were a number of students who needed a much deeper level of support. We developed a student support network that enabled joined-up thinking between the important people (SENDCo, Child Protection, Pastoral Leads, Counselling, Attendance) to meet the needs of those students. We also worked on our reflection room, the space that students were sent to if they could not meet our expectations in the classroom. The focus became on what was needed to reform those children. We provided tiers of support that offered timely and evidence-based intervention to do this.

In year two, we created Aspire, a school within a school, for the handful of students who were still struggling to meet expectations in the mainstream and needed more additional support. Aspire was kept entirely separate from the rest of the school. They had an adjusted school day with family dining and morning fitness. Alongside small-group teaching of core lessons led by subject specialists, they also had a bespoke pathway of intervention including, speech and language therapy, drama therapy, counselling, mentoring and literacy support. The aim was to provide a boost of positive behaviour support and curriculum, before slowly reintegrating them back into the main body of the school.

Where students have additional learning needs, it is always hard to find a balance between making reasonable adjustments without lowering expectations. Ultimately, it comes back to consistency. The students need a web of support in which all the adults have the same exceptions and warmly but firmly remind them when mistakes happen.

However, the landscape has changed a little since Covid-19. We are increasingly more concerned about the mental health of our young people it is always a fine balance; what do we pull them up on and what do we make exceptions for? Ultimately, though, good mental health benefits from calm, safe environments and clear boundaries, so maintaining high standards is vital.

A particular challenge around shifting a culture is where there is fear or parental complaints or Ofsted scrutiny. This can be really difficult, especially for heads, with whom the buck ultimately stops. There can be a high level of scrutiny where wholesale changes have been made. Leaders' hands are often tied and striking the balance between maintaining consistency and listening and responding to the legitimate needs and concerns of the community is always hard. However, as a behaviour/safeguarding lead, I know that when we bow too much, it creates far bigger problems.

Celebrating success is key in shifting a culture. Our school values were high and repeatedly on the agenda. Our house and merit system was all built around this. We constantly hammered the message home. We celebrated students' achievement and improvement in relation to these values in assemblies and sent postcards home (which the kids had designed themselves and loved). We held regular competitions, performances and cultural events all linked to the house system. After an initial period of ensuring the students understood and followed the new system, we had to ensure they felt appreciated, and this came through the house system, values and co-curricular programme.

Aspire very much had a family environment. This was important for building a sense of self-worth and belonging amongst a really vulnerable set of young people. They had a daily scoring system, which was linked to bespoke targets and tiered support. There were daily, weekly and termly opportunities for celebration, and students graduating Aspire was publicly celebrated.

The size of the school also matters. It has been a tougher job making a similar change in a school with double the numbers. There is so much more variance in terms of classrooms, cultures, families. Furthermore, the number of safeguarding cases has been greater. This can mean that we spend a longer period being reactive rather than always doing the preventative work we know we need to.

As a result of Covid-19, we have seen soaring numbers of disclosures and mental health concerns, as well as attendance difficulties. It has been harder to gain momentum and constancy. We had 1.5 terms of new expectations, systems then we went into lockdown. Every time it feels like we have had to start again from scratch. Where we have made ground with one kid, we have to reset because at home they may have had fewer boundaries or have been abused or neglected. That said, we are getting there now. If you keep consistently delivering the same message, it gets through, and the result is a safer and more positive school culture.

# Professional Development

This theme of attending to how people feel as well as what works applies to everything. As Dix says, 'Culture eats strategy for breakfast' (2017, p. 2). A mindful approach to CPD is evidence informed, coherent, low stakes and realistic. People need to believe it will work to get on board with it, and they have to feel safe in order to play about with their practice.

As a result, professional development needs to be held within a framework of knowledge about what works to improve teaching – both love *and* knowledge again. This is a challenge because as Mccrea points out, we do not have a clear conception of what expert teaching is (Mccrea, 2017). Fortunately, we do have Barak Rosenshine's *Principles of Instruction* (Rosenshine, 2012), which draw together Cognitive Science and the common features of high-performing teachers, to offer a robust insight into the art of teaching. These are illustrated clearly in Tom Sherington's excellent (2019) guide *Rosenshine's Principle's in Action*. Chapter 9 will look at some ways in which these principles might be brought to life in the classroom.

To lead teaching successfully, our leaders need to have strong mental models of what it means to be an expert teacher. This means they need the space to read, reflect and come together to discuss research and achieve consensus as to what they want to see in the classroom. Developing a shared language is key to this (Hutchinson, 2020). This language becomes the lifeblood of the culture. Another former colleague from Phoenix Academy John Kirkman (now vice principal at Mossbourne Victoria Park), developed the eight habits, which provided our team a language to translate and embed Rosenshine's principles into classroom practice. He explains his approach in the interview that follows.

---

**John Kirkman, Vice Principal at Mossbourne, Victoria Park, Discusses his Approach to Leading Teaching**

My thinking has not so much as changed but evolved since being at Mossbourne. The challenge at Phoenix was to help a novice (in terms of expertise in helping students to learn) staff body find the basics, grounded in research, and then apply these as the basis for their decision-making. Mossbourne has a much wider range of staff skill sets: from the extremely expert who get excellent results to mavericks who also get excellent results and a mix of novices and intermediate teachers.

I am a great believer in setting out the research in a way that people can access for their classroom. There are different approaches that can be taken to doing this. You could ask staff to prioritise reading research and hope they adapt their practice. We could tell them what to do without giving rationale from within the research, or we could find a middle ground. At Phoenix we called our approach The Habits. I have moved on in my thinking and am now calling them Principles. We give our Principles to staff as a founding document. We structure our CPD around thinking about and practising them. We use it as a tool to think about planning, delivering and reflecting on teaching and as a lens to evaluate practice.

Whilst we dramatically improved practice, we did not to get buy in fully at Phoenix. This was really important to me to do this at Mossbourne when I joined as Vice Principal. Essentially at Phoenix, I wrote The Habits. It was not a collaborative process. This was necessary because we did not have staff knowledge base to get everyone started in the first place. At Mossbourne, I have spent whole year with a teaching and learning team – made up of representatives of almost every subject area – developing our Principles. They look similar to the habits at Phoenix because we fed in the research but were collectively produced.

As a result of this, the implementation of them has been very successful. People are bought into the process and understand the research. Working alongside a wide range of subject leads has also allowed us to keep these principles open to the range of subjects, teachers' classrooms and children that will receive these principles, without shoehorning anyone into generic pedagogies. You cannot plan with just a maths or history classroom in mind. It needs to be for everybody.

The intention is that we are promoting practice rather than directing it. It has been powerful to have a psychology teacher on the team. She has strong knowledge of Cognitive Science. This knowledge base helps to ensure that we do not run away with things, like dual coding, and implement them poorly.

Our CPD programme is built around these principles. The sessions take a similar format. They begin with an exposition. The person leading explains and models the principle in question. The second half is focused on transforming this into teacher practice. This allows you to sell the reasons why you are promoting something and provide a model for how it might work in practice. Then time is given to digest this in subject groups.

Due to the pandemic, much of our CPD has had to happen in bubbles. We have recorded our training sessions on video, which are then played in classrooms, with Heads of Department facilitating. These conversations have been especially rich due to this shared subject base.

This really got me thinking about the forum in which we do CPD. Whole-school CPD can be powerful, but it is also big and noisy. We have found being in learning areas amongst peers is good way of doing it. At Phoenix we did not have the numbers and the expertise to make this happen. You must make sure the person leading CPD is an expert. They cannot have just read something on the internet. This requires careful thinking and long-term planning, as well as the right staff supporting delivery.

When I joined Mossbourne, I had a three-year plan. In year one the intention was to make sure everyone was brought up to speed on the evidence and to construct The Principles. In the second year we launched The Principles and got everyone on board. Next year, year three, will be more mixed. There will be some whole-school training, but it will be much more bespoke.

I have done a lot of thinking about how you can empower people. It is all good training teachers, but they must feel they can use it in a way that works for them in their classroom. Checklists have a place in extreme circumstances, but they quickly become useless and end up being disempowering. How you make a policy alive in peoples' classrooms is what matters.

We have teachers who are mavericks and do things like big, seemingly unplanned class debates that I would advise others not to. However, because they are personable, charismatic and know their subjects inside out and backwards, they can get away with it and the students thrive.

When I started at Mossbourne, there was a range of alignment to the evidence. Now people cohere much more around it. We still have novices and mavericks, and that is okay. We take the best bits from those mavericks.

You must have a policy and CPD programme that allows those people to be themselves. It needs to be responsive, not downloaded from the internet. It is hard for leaders who want things to fit into neat boxes to cope with maverick teachers. Not everything can be reduced to an infographic on one side of A4. There is something intangible about some great teachers' classrooms and great practice, but it includes knowledge, love of the kids and experience. The question is how we make space for those people at the same time as not undermining the evidence and research.

You have to be conformable with being uncomfortable if leading teaching at a school. In a perfect world, everybody's coachable. For some teachers, it is not going to happen next week. Certainly everyone is able to improve their practice, and as Dylan Williams says, we have to learn to work with the teachers we have got rather than expecting a new batch to come round the corner and save the day. However, there are also real children in front of us whose lives can be affected by poor teaching. You have to be sensible and thoughtful and ethical, and you have to quickly improve some people's practice for the good of the students.

I do not believe in a pure peer-coaching model. I think that most schools that say they do that do other things covertly. At Mossbourne, everyone observes everyone, but also, managers provide ongoing and intensive support.

It is important how you frame observation. It is okay to identify your novices who need extra support but not to 'set' teachers. This is just grading by proxy and is not helpful. High-stakes accountability creates a culture of fear. However, there needs to be a low-stakes observation culture but not a no-stakes one. Otherwise, we do a disservice to our students. We have to respond to where the school is and the needs to the children and community. Sometimes that requires being tough; sometimes that means loosening a little.

When I arrived the school, they had removed grades and gone straight to peer observations only. It needed some protocols to enable a low-stakes culture to thrive. I reintroduced management observations alongside an action-steps protocol. This guided the observer with giving feedback. This structure enables observation to feel low stakes but still did the job of flagging up who needs support.

Senior leaders trained the middle leaders to do this. I want people to be observed in their subject area, as the more barriers there are for the observer, the more feedback becomes watered down. Then we end up relying on proxies for what great teaching is rather than getting to the nuance.

I believe nuance and decision-making are the two things that make great teaching. I want my teachers to be thinking, 'What decisions were made in the classroom?' 'What was the impact?' and 'What else could they have decided?' Nuance is interconnected with this. When we stop and ask a teacher, why did you ask that question there? Why is that a great decision? When would you not do it like that? That is the nuance.

Too often we try to do too many things and lose sight of our CPD priorities. We constantly receive emails advertising all sorts of training, and they all sound so tempting. However, we need to be careful not to overload our teams or undermine our aims with inconsistent messaging. CPD needs to hang together in a coherent framework, which allows staff at all levels to build mental models of what success looks like in their job. Whilst the aim is to reduce complexity in this way, we need to be careful not to shoehorn our teachers into generic pedagogy by insisting on too much consistency. We must take a middle way, keeping in mind our shared goals and respecting and developing the expertise of subject specialists. This is done through trust and time, allowing subject leaders autonomy and teams plenty of the CPD allocation to expand their subject knowledge and discuss scholarship within their disciplines.

The Uncommon Schools resources provide another helpful template for developing a shared language which is broad and adaptable enough to avoid being reduced to generic pedagogy. The *Teach Like a Champion*, or TLAC (Lemov, 2014), techniques are, similarly to Rosenshine's principles, the distillation of the practice of master teachers. Whilst the techniques in and of themselves are not the answer, they are a fantastic jumping-off point for beginner-teacher education and CPD. Also of Uncommon Schools, Paul Bambrick-Santoyo's (2016) *Get Better Faster* provides a coherent curriculum for new or struggling teachers, breaking down the constituent parts of classroom management, focusing on the highest-impact classroom strategies first.

His earlier book *Leverage Leadership* (2012) is particularly helpful in providing a model, instructional coaching, for how this might be translated into practice. Jon Hutchinson (2020) likens the instructional coaching approach to that of a sports coach. Just like a coach watches their team and breaks the steps for improvement into meaningful and actionable chunks, the teacher coach watches the coachees and suggests 'action steps'. These are then agreed on between coach and coachee, who then practice these steps through role play before implementing them in the classroom. This is low stakes; it is not linked to performance management or ranked in any way. It is solely focused on what is going to make the most difference for that class.

In the best schools, everyone has a coach, no matter their seniority or experience, because all of us can improve. When there is a shared commitment to learning, then the fear of someone coming into your classroom and judging you is taken away. This is when Myatt's concept of management by wandering around (2016) really comes into its element. If leaders habitually drop into lessons and have conversations with colleagues about teaching practice, then there really is no need to grade people against a checklist or store their progress on a spreadsheet. You know your teachers and the areas they need to work on, and more importantly so do they.

A strong network of middle leaders supports this, but the aim is ultimately to remove the hierarchy whilst preserving a respect for expertise. Some of the best leaders I have worked with very early in my career encouraged me to see them teach. This was not because I was a better teacher than them; in fact, they probably took my feedback with a pinch of salt. However, seeing their expertise in action and being given the opportunity to think deeply alongside an expert about why it worked helped to demystify their expertise. Plus, a fresh pair of eyes, however inexperienced, will usually offer some insight. You never know who your teachers will be. The paradox at the heart of the notion of being an expert is that everyone can always get better, even a master.

## Curriculum and Assessment

The binary that pits knowledge against skills has created fault lines in the educational discourse. I am an unashamed advocate of a powerful knowledge-rich curriculum and think it is unhelpful that this conversation has become associated with right-wing politics.

Under pressure to get results, many schools have become exam factories. So for me it is a real relief that we are now thinking about what our students know and assessing them in terms of their mastery of that content rather than generic skills mapped back from exam specifications. A focus on curriculum helps us move away from busy generic tasks to more intentional classroom practice and allows us to build real challenge and rigour into the learning experience.

## Challenge

One finding of cognitive load theory is that we remember what we give attention to, or as Willingham puts it, memory is 'the residue of thought' (2008–2009, p. 18). Therefore, it is desirable that students struggle a little with the intrinsic load, the subject content of our lessons. However, we do not want them to be distracted by unnecessary thinking about the nature of the activity or who they are sitting next to.

This intrinsic load should have a 'desirable amount of difficulty', a sort of Goldilocks amount. Without challenge, we cannot acquire new knowledge nor develop resilience. Yet too much and we become overwhelmed. The mindful teacher knows exactly how much cognitive challenge their students need and how to frame it so they feel safe enough to try and, if need be, fail and try again. Challenge and scaffolding should be built into long-term curriculum plans, in order to steadily increase the level of difficulty and decrease the level of support across a young person's journey in school.

Reorienting ourselves away from the generic and towards our subjects frees us from a focus on performance. When we think deeply about our curriculum, we start to consider what our students' knowledge entitlement is – that is, what we want them to walk away from our subjects, remembering and being able to apply in the world beyond school.

## Sequencing

Therefore, our curriculums need to be built with memory in mind. So the sequencing of the curriculum is key. Counsell describes curriculum as narrative (2018), whilst Neil Almond (2020) uses the analogy of a box set. He suggests that like in a series, where overarching plots and subplots tie episodes and seasons together, a curriculum, too, should have 'plots' that build together into a web of knowledge.

When we reframe curriculum in this way *as* the progression model, assessment becomes something meaningful, not simply a grade for us to input into a spreadsheet or a proverbial stick to beat children with. We can begin to have conversations that makes sense with students, parents, teachers and leaders alike about what children know and what they need to further understand or develop. In the following case study, Corinne Flett talks about what this might look like in practice.

**Corinne Flett, Vice Principal at a Large Inner London Academy, Talks About Curriculum, Assessment and the High-Stakes Nature of the Exam System**

Curriculum is the keystone of education. Without it nothing else stands up. The purpose of schools, and particularly an academy like ours, is to give students an education that they wouldn't get otherwise. Without a considered, well-sequenced, quality-assured curriculum, you can have good behaviour, good pastoral care and sometimes even decent results but you still won't be providing the true education these children deserve for now and for their future. What they deserve is to be taught *the best of which has been thought and said* and, for many students, to be taught the knowledge that their advantaged peers already get from home, trips and travel. The only way we can achieve this is by putting curriculum front and centre.

I believe that problems in the current system are twofold. One is that results and league tables have become the primary driver for some leadership teams. Decisions are made with only this in mind, and it can distract us from what we know is fundamentally good teaching and learning. But I'll come back to that later. The other problem is one that Amanda Spielman highlighted in 2017. 'There was a time (long ago) when teachers were taught the theory that underpins curriculum planning. Over time, this competence across the sector ebbed away. This may be because it was generally not thought to be so important after the establishment of a national curriculum' (Spielman, 2017). This makes sense. If you are being told what to teach and not thinking about how to teach it, your perception of 'teaching' becomes distorted. It is a common mistake for a department to ask only experienced teachers to write schemes of work because they believe less experienced staff cannot do it, but this can happen over and over again. Then expertise is never developed. Research tells us that the most effective teachers understand sequencing and Cognitive Science. They use their understanding of student misconceptions to drive learning forward. Teachers will never develop this if they are not allowed to write curriculum themselves and learn from the eternally iterative process of curriculum development.

Unfortunately, the National Curriculum took these experiences away. That's why I think we got to this place where some said, 'Those that can do and those that can't teach.' I've certainly been told that during my career. When I started teacher training, we were using off-the-shelf schemes of work, printing and handing out worksheets without even understanding ourselves what was on them. Completion of the worksheet was the aim, and if this happened, then *obviously* learning had taken place. Completed worksheets marked out of 10 stuck into ever-thickening exercise books were considered good teaching; they were poor proxies and missed the point. Now we ask our teachers, 'Are you thinking about the activity or thinking about the thinking?' Planning centres around what students are thinking rather than what they are outputting, and as a leader, you have to get beneath the skin of each subject to really see this.

One way to address the gap in curriculum expertise is by using CPD for curriculum enactment. Andy Nichols, AP Teaching & Learning, has been working on this at our academy. We know that CPD is more effective if it is subject specific, not generic. We have all sat through a didactic session on 'questioning' where outcomes depend entirely upon the ingenuity, reflection and motivation of each individual teacher and experienced teachers feel they are being taught to *suck eggs*. Instead we think it is more powerful for teachers to really understand the thinking process behind curriculum decisions. I have never been able to teach a lesson I haven't written because I don't know the thought process behind it, and it's the same for curriculum. Our sessions centre around a scheme of work that a number of members of staff are teaching. The person who has written the scheme launches it. They explain the purpose, the context, potential misconceptions and barriers and, most crucially, the sequence; what students learned before it and what will come after. Then teachers start teaching the scheme. Halfway through, they meet again to look at the books and talk it through. For example, they might say, 'I changed the order of these lessons because that made more sense to me.' This open dialogue allows us to develop the best possible curriculum enactment. I might write a scheme of work with a sequence that makes sense to me but no one else. All feedback is useful in developing the best scheme possible. The final curriculum-enactment session provides a space for teachers to reflect on the scheme as a whole and look at it in relation to book work and the assessment. A record is created of changes that need to be made collaboratively during gained time. And this process repeats itself each term until these conversations become commonplace both within and outside of CPD time. A well-written curriculum will support a teacher, but it is not going to define them. Great teachers bring curriculum alive through the minute-to-minute and lesson-to-lesson decisions they make in the classroom, but these decisions are only impactful if they are well informed. This speaks to the interconnectedness of curriculum and pedagogy. It is not either or.

When it comes to assessing the impact of curriculum and the effectiveness of teaching, the fair way is to triangulate: lesson observations, conversations with students and teachers, and scrutiny of student work and evaluative data. Dylan William has talked about how observational ratings of teachers can dramatically shift depending on context. Usually, observed teachers are rated more highly with higher-attaining groups due to unconscious observer bias. When I was Head of Department, I managed a teacher who would get very flustered in observations. External observers would suggest that she wasn't good enough, but I knew she was. Her students respected her, they were driven by her passion for biology, their exam results were good, work in their books was strong but she once said 'stuff' instead of 'equipment', and for one observer, that was enough to write her off. This highlights the need to triangulate, but triangulation takes time and so rarely happens. This is where the new Ofsted deep dives seem well designed. They allegedly 'test to destruction'. Is the quality of education good in this area, and where is the proof for this beyond teacher observation? Like many schools, we conduct a similar process internally, not because it is how Ofsted do it but because it makes sense. It is a mammoth task that takes weeks, but I think it throws up school and departmental trends that really help us improve.

After a series of deep dives, we get together as an SLT to share trends and explore what are whole-school priorities and what are departmental. This requires us as leaders to have strong subject knowledge. It is hard to know how to measure something without really embedding yourself within it. If you stand on the side line, use only binary grading systems and try to hold people to account, you will never do it fairly and productively. This chimes with Counsell's ideas about senior leadership of curriculum. A very current example would be the need for SLT to understand that a music department approach to 'Covid-19 catch-up' is going to be very, very different to English. What we know, thanks to Counsell, is that as SLT, you've got to get deep within your departments. This requires putting the hours in to upskill yourself. Perhaps it is a generational thing. In previous years at our academy, the job of SLT appeared to be to measure outcomes, not the curriculum. As the next generation of Heads of Department, who have more experience writing curriculum, move into SLT, they will have even more understanding and therefore depth than we do.

There is, of course, a place for data, but the word 'purpose' has to be the key word in any assessment strategy. You need to know why you are assessing. Too often we run assessments and get information but then do not use it for anything. Different assessments have different purposes. I categorise them as formative, summative and evaluative.

Many colleagues have argued about semantics here, but for me the distinction between summative and evaluative assessment is not always highlighted despite being very important. For me, summative assessment measures progress against the curriculum while evaluative compares data to national benchmarks. Mistakes have been made when schools collect evaluative data too frequently. We have all heard a head of department complain that the next data entry point has come around before lessons taken from the previous data point have been implemented. It's okay to assess students for evaluative data, but not when this distorts the purpose and gets in the way of measurement and action against the taught curriculum. There should be room for assessment against the curriculum used at a classroom or departmental level to allow quick response to gaps or areas of weakness. We might respond in different ways. If it is light touch, perhaps you only need to focus a series of 'do now' questions on the topic, but perhaps a whole section needs reteaching, or it may even be used as the rationale to rewrite schemes of work or the long-term curriculum – whatever can be done to enhance student learning moving forwards.

It's obvious that external accountability and exam results are important, but they too often distort what should be the true aim of education. This has been exposed over the last two years with centre- and teacher-assessed grades. Whilst this process has been truly horrendous in terms of staff workload, I think there have been some benefits for the profession, namely more trust. This was a necessary, overdue development as we need to trust the teacher's ability to communicate to parents accurately and honestly where their child is in relation to expectations. I would like to be able to just give a report to parents that says the child is 'working at or above expectations' or 'working below expectations', but because of the historic lack of trust, teachers reports seem to only be accepted if they are filled with numbers. The frustration for teachers is that these numbers can often not truly reflect student ability, can be arbitrary or, more commonly, are completely misunderstood by the parent. Ideally you would replace reports altogether with parents' evenings, a two-way conversation, but again time is the issue.

What was particularly unhelpful last year was the media reporting that exams were 'cancelled' where the reality was quite different. Almost all schools replaced exams with exams. However, the variety of quality assurance was wild, and there was no practical way to rein this in. Inevitably, some schools gamed the system, and as a result, you can't push a system of teacher assessment forward because it is too unfair, particularly to the disadvantaged. But traditional exams are the same. There was a question one year in a physics paper about the circuit between light switches at the top and bottom of the stairs. The question asked why this was a useful circuit. Having marked a number of incorrect answers to this question, I thought, if you don't live in a house, you won't have any idea why that's useful. A few years ago, I also remember an incredibly talented young man who was on track for excellent grades but, because of where he lived, got beaten up the night before his English literature exam. He turned up for the exam despite being in no fit state to take it – there was no other viable option available to him. It's an example of how privilege is inadvertently baked into the system. It will take a lot to create an exam system that doesn't disadvantage disadvantaged kids. And so, if both centre-assessed grades and formal examination disadvantage certain groups, we've got to think of another way to hold all schools to account fairly.

When looking at case studies of specific young people, we are reminded how much the odds are stacked against some of them. Teacher bias is just one challenge; the huge amount of support required for each individual is another. Covid-19 and lockdown has further exposed this. Despite common media reports, the gap was not just about technology; it was far more complex than that. We had year 11s who missed weeks of online lessons because they spent most of the lockdown looking after their siblings. They had the technology needed, they wanted to attend but these things are so out of their – or even the families' – control. Some students have come back to us with real mental health issues, an increase in self-harm and suicidal ideation, increase in inappropriate sexual contact or remarks and a negative outlook as the whole world tells them that they have fallen behind and need to work harder than their predecessors due to a situation they couldn't control. Internally we are trying to change the narrative on this and offer as much support as we can, so our job right now is to do even more with less.

Unfortunately, when a school is placed on a league table or criticised for its results, attention is drawn away from the more important elements of education that I have described. We start to lose sight of what really matters and overcomplicate at the expense of staff and student well-being. Of course the government needs a device to push educational standards higher, but we also know it is possible to appear to push your own standards higher by creating an exam factory and putting certain students in certain qualifications even if that is not in the best interests of the individual student. I would argue that there are very few schools at the top of league tables that do not have some angle in trying to play the system, be it through aggressive Y11 after-school intervention, careful curation of qualifications offered, last-minute disapplication or some other device. And you can't blame schools for doing this because once results appear good enough, the threat of punitive accountability is removed, and a school can finally get on with the fundamentals that make the educational offer great. In the current system, as my former head teacher would say, the *tail is wagging the dog*, and until schools or trusts are brave enough to ignore the league tables, really listen to teachers and see through the fog of accountability-created hoop jumping the system won't change.

## Subject-Specific CPD

To get curriculum right requires investing in our teachers' subject knowledge. It is important to be clear on the core disciplinary and substantive knowledge you want all students to master. However, the curriculum should not become a straitjacket. Do not be scared if lessons veer a little off script. When teachers have strong subject expertise, this builds what Counsell describes as the 'hinterland' (Counsell, 2018) – the rich reservoir of knowledge that brings the curriculum to life.

We want our students to feel their teachers' passion and expertise. Of course, to be able to convey this passion authentically, you do have to really love your subject. Specification-driven teaching and generic pedagogy stripped this away for many of us for a time. However, subject-specific CPD – be that tailor-made courses, engaging with academic research or simply listening to radio shows and podcasts (like *In Our Time*) – has the power to re-enliven this. Mary Myatt has gathered together an excellent section of resources on the subject links' section of her website.[1]

This cannot be a quick fix or something that teachers should be expected to undertake in their own time. Developing teachers' subject knowledge should be something that is invested in and honed over time as part of a coherent CPD offer.

## Resourcing

This reorientation towards the content of lessons and away from the activities is also freeing in terms of workload. Once you have invested in quality resources, they can be used time and time again. So there should be no more time spent cutting up card sorts or creating PowerPoints from scratch.

Kit Howard makes a strong case for moving away from PowerPoint, altogether which she describes as being 'dull and distracting in equal measure' (Howard, 2020, p. 137). She suggests it does not actually support a more manageable workload as 'whilst it promises' to provide a starting point for teachers, it can actually become more of an onerous task to make use of it' (*ibid*, p. 136). Often a lot of work needs to be done to decipher the thinking behind a PowerPoint.

It also does teaching down by implying that 'teachers can be teachers simply by putting an explanatory screen behind themselves'. It seems to be that the period of remote learning due to Covid-19 has revealed how much this not the case and how it is our most vulnerable students who most need their teacher's presence. A shift away from PowerPoints forces us to remember that a presentation is not the lesson itself; it is the teacher that brings any resources to life. There are many curriculum artifacts that are helpful in delivering a knowledge rich approach, but they should not be confused with the knowledge itself. Booklets, textbooks and knowledge organisers can all help to crystallise a teacher's thinking through the planning process and enable complex information to be presented to students in a straightforward and coherent way. Ideally these will contain opportunities to engage with primary sources in your subject. These may build disciplinary knowledge – for example, engaging with historical scholarship in History or substantive knowledge by, for example, looking at sacred texts in Religious Studies.

Streamlined resources focus on the core of what you want students to know and strip back the frills and distraction as much as possible. Applying the principle of cognitive load theory, Howard suggests if you do use PowerPoint, streamline it to reinforce 'one key message' by being selective about the information that you chose to put in it. The hinterland (Counsell, 2018) can be worked in through teacher's expertise live in the classroom.

PowerPoint has become a crutch for some teachers (as textbooks were before them), taking them away from responsive teaching and into their own performance, particularly if our subject knowledge is not good enough. However, with strong subject-led CPD, teachers can be freed to *be* in the room and really respond to their students.

## Perversions of Assessment

In his acclaimed book *Responsive Teaching*, Harry Fletcher-Wood (2018) explores the perversions of notions of formative assessment or assessment for learning (AfL). He suggests that these terms have become inadequate because a misguided understanding of what they mean has become common practice. Fletcher-Wood attributes his (self-confessed) own poor use of AfL in the past to the focus on techniques in his training rather than there being an understanding of the principles behind it.

This resonates strongly with my own experience. He reminds us of the absurdity of National Curriculum levels, exacerbated by a context of out-of-control monitoring and accountability. Giving the example of a level descriptor in history, 'Level 5, Student begins to make links between causes', Fletcher-Wood suggests that the prioritisation of generic skills left us 'simply tracking pupils progress towards target levels' (Fletcher-Wood, 2018). The dangerous combination of applying the logic of exams and neglecting the role of subject knowledge in the formation of these skills meant assessment dominated everything but gave us very little useful information about how to really move pupils on (Fletcher-Wood, 2018).

In my experience, there were, however, plenty of techniques to demonstrate AfL (lolly sticks, reams of writing on mini white boards, traffic lights and, of course, tons of marking). The thinking behind them, though, was less commonly explored. In the context of high-stakes accountability, perversions emerged out of even the most sensible techniques. With progress desperately needing to be proved to every observer, stickers were placed on the front of books, and students were cajoled, coached and spoon-fed into articulating the likes of 'I am a level five. To move to a level six, I need to make links between causes', all this without any real understanding of what that meant or the subject knowledge to really respond well to the information gathered.

Reams of secondary data, spreadsheets on spreadsheets, were then built on this core of inaccurate primary data and sometimes used as a stick to beat people with. No wonder so many of my former colleagues just made up the data. 'Just ensure that they make progress in line with the flight path' was the advice I was given when, wet behind the ears, I dared to question the emperor's new clothes that was National Curriculum Levels.

## Responsive Teaching

Fletcher-Wood suggests we might instead use the concept of responsive teaching to help us avoid these distortions. This rebranding shifts the purpose of assessment towards identifying what students have learnt in order to do something about it.

For this to happen, the curriculum needs to be rigorous and well sequenced (*ibid.*, p6). The curriculum, not exam skills, needs to be the progression model. Assessment must be focused on the specifics of what students are leaning rather than testing generic skills. Furthermore, we must accept that students' learning is unpredictable; it cannot always fit onto a nice linear flight path. Once we recognise this, we continue Evans' 'waltz', working to simplify and reduce that complexity (2020a, p. 229). One way of doing this is to ask how we can make our assessments yield better information about where students are in relation to the curriculum. Then we must have accountability systems that reflect this rather than the other way round. This requires us as leaders to have a strong level of subject knowledge and allow plenty of CPD time both to communicate this thinking to teachers and allow them to develop more effective assessment tools.

## Meaningful Use of Data

If we are going to ask students and teachers to go to the effort of gathering data about where students are, we must do something meaningful with it. This applies at all levels of school: from staff surveys to reading tests to in class questioning. I once inherited a SEND department that had spent a fortune on educational psychology (EP) assessments, but they had never communicated any of the findings to teachers, let alone integrated them into their teaching and learning strategy. I think the principle of minimalism applies here: we should be doing just a few things really well. Rather than exerting loads of effort gathering information that will never be used, think carefully about what data you want to gather and then overuse it. In the case of the EP, I chose to use one of our assessment slots to have a preliminary meeting with the psychologist to explain our approach to teaching and intervention. This meant they were able to suggest feedback on our approach and provide strategies for young people that aligned with this. In addition, we digested the reports provided into non-SEND specialist language and presented them with strategies to the young persons' parents and class teachers. We then held regular reviews to explore the success of the strategies and ditched anything that was not working.

## Powerful Knowledge

Whilst I am an advocate of a knowledge-rich curriculum, this does not mean I wish to teach decontextualised facts or for students to regurgitate what I teach them verbatim. This is a fundamental misunderstanding of a powerful knowledge approach. By giving students a well-sequenced and varied curriculum, we are giving them a set of tools to understand and access the world on their own terms.

Paraphrasing Audre Lorde (1984), I have written before about what I see as the revolutionary potential of powerful knowledge, to provide our students the tools, the knowledge of how 'the master's house' works so that they can dismantle it (Reid, 2018). That is by exposing the truths of the world we live in, in all their beauty and messiness; we give our students a window to many worlds and crucially allow them to feel they have a stake in it. In this way, knowledge is not dead but something in process that calls one to action. What is more, skills and knowledge are not a binary but two sides of the same coin. Skills, or procedural knowledge, are crucial in this metaphorical house demolition. We want children to be able to apply what they learn in the classroom independently. An example of this might be if, through a joined-up and intelligent Science and Geography curriculum, we successfully introduce our students to the magnificence, complexity and threats faced by this planet it is likely that they will feel the call to arms to protect it.

However, we must recognise not all learning is cerebral. There are many forms and ways of knowing and being in the world. If young people do not have a relationship with nature and their only experiences of the natural world come from inside the classroom, their ability to bring to life what they learn will be limited.

## Co-curricular

Therefore, returning to the notion of the middle way, a rigorous academic curriculum needs to be balanced with opportunities for different kinds of learning – one that is less structured, outdoors and more physical. At Phoenix our ethos was built on the notion of two pillars, the curricular and the co-curricular. Alongside a knowledge-rich classroom experience, children were provided with opportunities to undertake multiple forms of adventure learning, from whole-year-group orienteering activities to a select group that climbed Ben Nevis in the winter.

The transformative potential of this – particularly for students from very urban environments who may have never even walked on uneven ground, let alone spent a night under canvas – cannot be underestimated. This provision was not limited to one-off expeditions; an extended day provided a youth club for all KS3 children, which offered a range of sports and creative activities. Not only did this provide our students access to experiences that they would have not usually had and build that ephemeral 'character' that schools are supposed to teach. It also provided an opportunity for a positive intermingling between the school and the wider community. Furthermore, this extended day functioned as a protective factor for some of our more vulnerable students, serving to make the pull of school a bit more alluring than that of the street. It must however be noted that none of this is easy in times of austerity, when budgets are squeezed all round.

## Community

In the hubbub of our schools, accountable as we are to more demanding masters like Ofsted, we can temporarily forget that they are located in and serve communities. Mindful leaders think about what the school is used for after hours. They ask, 'How is it serving the community?' Are lettings simply seen as an opportunity to make money in hard times, or are they a way of engaging with and supporting the wider community?

Research from the Education Endowment Fund (2019) indicates that parental engagement is one of the key levers of student attainment. There are a number of schools successfully integrating partnerships with families and other community organisations into the ethos of their schools. At Capital City Academy in West London, the fantastic organisation Salusbury World runs a range of sessions for asylum seekers and refugee families, providing hubs that offer a range of support, from English lessons to migration status support. The Reach Children's Hub in Feltham has honed a similar model, an explanation of which is in Chapter 7.

With this in mind, how we engage with the web of support that sits behind schools (from cleaning to printer maintenance to deliveries) matters. They are our community too. Mary Myatt reminds us that every interaction with a supplier or member of support staff is an opportunity to live and breathe the school's ethos (2016, p. 71). Not only is this just the right thing to do, but it provides a wonderful model for our students of how to treat everyone in society.

## Joy

Chapter 5 is dedicated to how we build a culture of respect and learning across a school, and this chapter has emphasised the deep work over the frivolous. Nevertheless, mindful leaders do not forget the power of playfulness. Remember the healthy mind platter? We all need non-goal-oriented time, and so social events have a small but powerful role to play in facilitating this culture too.

Like most things, such events have a hidden curriculum. How social occasions are handled speaks to the leadership's attitude towards its staff body.

## Some Questions to Ask About Social Events

- Is time made for them at significant points in the year?

- Does everyone get invited? Are they inclusive? For example do they take place in a pub, which might exclude Muslim colleagues?

- Does everyone include the support and contracted staff?

- Are the leadership part of it or seen to be separate?

As a leader, your every move is scrutinised, and the smallest gestures can make or break a culture. If the leadership team sticks to 'their own' at social events, it sends a very powerful message; so does a leadership team who is prepared to have a metaphorical drink with their staff. You do not need to be everyone's friend, and it is not a bad idea to sneak out of the party before the drinking gets too raucous and you hear something you might not want to. Nonetheless, making an effort in this way matters. It goes a long way to helping you become seen as approachable. As usual, though, this cannot be forced. People sense what you feel about them and whether you really want to be there. So a genuine will to hang out with your staff from time to time matters.

## Summary

- Build time in into the school culture and your leadership practice to allow for **engagement with research,** to **listen** to the **school community** and to provide **space to reflect** on what is working and what can be streamlined.

- This helps **prioritise deep learning** and steer us away from quick fixes and lethal mutations.

- Get **systems** *and* **relationships** right.

- Strip back those things that do not make a difference, and focus on the core work of **curriculum** and **teaching**.

- Invest in **meaningful professional-development** approaches, like instructional coaching, that are focused on the acquisition of subject knowledge and approaches proven to have an impact, such as Rosenshine's principles and the TLAC techniques.

- There is significant power in **engaging well** with the wider school **community**.

## Note

1 www.marymyatt.com/subject-links.

# 7 Radical Inclusion

This chapter will do the following:

- Outline some of the challenges and paradoxes of inclusion
- Use a case study to expound what the impact of this might be on an individual life course
- Suggest models for working based on the practices of exemplary schools

## Inclusion at the Core

If the purpose of Mindfulness is to enable compassionate social action, then mindful leadership must also sit within a framework of moral purpose. That is, it should aim to transform society towards equality by bringing the most vulnerable or marginalised at the heart of what we do. That means we need to start with considering what our more needy students might require and how we can ensure that a diversity of perspectives are included in our schools. This covers all areas of school leadership: ethos, curriculum, pedagogy. The paradox of this approach, that has diversity and inclusion at its heart, is that everyone benefits.

The previous chapters have emphasised that staff and students are not so different. To flourish, we all need to feel securely attached to our schools and there may be times, to use the language of Dixons Trinity Academy, where any one of us might need rescuing from a mountain. This notion is at the core of leading mindfully. Inclusion must never be an add on or an afterthought. As a SENDCo, I used to say that my aim was to make myself redundant. Discounting that as a statutory role that would never happen, the premise of removing barriers so additional support is no longer needed stands.

If we look at additional needs through a social – rather than medical – lens, then we can see how both the conditions of someone's early experiences and the school and home environment shape the extent to which someone is enabled or disabled. This is why an understanding of attachment theory can be so helpful. The

DOI: 10.4324/9781003198482-10

suggestions in the previous chapter go a long way to creating the culture and systems that ensure this. However, at risk of undermining my own point that inclusion should be built in, rather than have its own chapter, I want to speak to some of the specific challenges that might arise when we work to include those with disadvantages and/or protected characteristics. Namely the role of disability, racism, classism and poverty, sexism and other forms of othering (or trauma) in shaping students (and staff's) experience and how a mindful approach to inclusion might respond to this.

## Systemic Inequalities

Core to addressing multiple disadvantages that intersect is taking a systemic view. We can divide things up and label them, 'ASD', 'pastoral', 'mental health', 'low literacy', as much as we want but in my experience most of the pastoral and academic challenges that we face in schools, aside from the ones that result from systems that do not work properly, centre around a handful of problems: poverty; trauma and marginalisation. Remember the brain scans that showed remarkable similarities in lack of integration in a wide range of conditions? This is not to be reductive about additional needs, these challenges pan out in different ways and we must know our students as individuals.

Nevertheless, at the heart of many of our young people's problems are systemic and intersecting issues, poor housing, neglect, mental and physical ill health, addiction, family breakdown and communication challenges. What are referred to as 'wicked problems' due to their complex and interconnected nature? These problems are often cumulative and iterative. They take on a life of their own as the individual or family interacts with the world around them and, unfortunately disadvantages often compound each other in multiple domains a once. The notion of the 'Mathew Effect' was coined by Keith Stanovich (1986) to explain how early reading success leads to further reading success later in life. This is because children who do well in reading read more and vice versa. The notion of 'social thinning' is a similar concept but refers to the way that those who begin with more social capital can more easily accumulate it than their peers (McCrory, 2020).

## A Story

These phenomena are perhaps best explained in this fictional, but all too real, vignette of the formative years of a young person. Let us call him Kai. Whilst Kai's mother, Amber, is pregnant, she experiences high levels of stress due to what is described as the 'toxic triangle' of substance misuse, domestic violence and mental illness.

Both the stress hormone, cortisol, and the alcohol reach Kai in-utero. As a result, when he is born it is harder for him to settle. Therefore, Amber is extra-exhausted, and as well as continuing to be abused, she finds it difficult to bond with Kai. Kai learns that he is often not responded to if he cries. What is more if he is responded to, he is often met by an angry or frustrated face.

As a result, he develops an internal working model that sees others as untrustworthy and his self as unworthy of love. Due to this, it is more difficult for Kai to build relationships, leading to less social interaction, exposure to language and limited curiosity. His Early Years Setting raises their concerns to social services and identify him as having SEND. This means he has additional support but some of his teachers also lower their expectations of what he can do compared to his peers, and because of the way SEND funding is used in his school, he has more time with a teaching assistant than a qualified teacher.

Amber lives in poverty and works several zero-hours contracts to pay the bills. The result of this financial insecurity and unpredictable working pattern is she is not able to work alongside the school or social services and she has no time or energy to read or even talk much with Kai at home. His nutrition also suffers. At school and when he is unsupervised in the community, Kai 'acts out', he tries to find belonging in other ways and mask some of his vulnerabilities. This leaves Kai exposed to grooming and criminal exploitation. In time, he gets caught up with gangs and the youth justice system. This not only compounds his increasing mental health challenges but also makes it harder for him to get a job once he has a criminal record. The frustrations and patterns set up by this situation lead to a cycle of mental ill-health, addiction and violence which are eventually handed on to the next generation.

This heart-breaking story is just a story but the themes are all too common. The Mental Health Commission's (2011) study indicates that the shame and instability of being poor exposes communities to multiple psychological and material vulnerabilities. These challenges can then also be compounded by racism and other prejudices.

It is both a real reminder why our job matters and also speaks to the vastness of what we are dealing with. The paradox is that we cannot locate the problem in the individual or family but it is also where we must start. What is more, as schools we must recognise our limitations. In the context of austerity, schools are increasingly asked to do more but we cannot do everything; our primary purpose is – and must be – to educate. Yet we still have a role to play in supporting Kai and Amber and those like them. Let us explore what that might look like.

## Protective Factors

If school can be a safe base, it can be a hugely protective and even mitigating factor. To ensure this, as mindful leaders we must also give attention to our own role in reproducing or entrenching some of these inequalities. Be that through ignorance, prejudice or low expectations. This is particularly important, if we are working in poor and ethnically diverse communities, as we know school leadership is still overwhelmingly white, middle class and male. Whilst this is not going to change overnight, if we have a seat at the table, we need to do what we can to in invite to that table, a plurality of voices that includes those that make up the communities we serve. Once we have them involved, we must be reflective enough to listen and learn from them, and then crucially put that learning into action.

Too often our responses to the concerns of our communities are reactive and bolt on, a result of fear. This can lead to lethal mutations that actually make things worse, in the long run, for the very people we are trying to improve things for. Our high-stakes accountability system sets atomised, often competing targets that exacerbate or draw our attention from the inequalities that plague our society rather than fix them. As a result, we can become focused on protecting ourselves, distracted by the symptoms rather than the roots of problem.

## Expectations

The power of our expectations to shape the lives of the students we teach should be recognised. Unfortunately, studies (Ferguson, 2003; Burgess, 2009; Gilliam et al., 2016) routinely demonstrate that, from pre-school age, teachers underestimate the attainment of, and more harshly discipline, black students. This rightly deserves scrutiny.

Yet race is not the only area where teacher expectations or assumptions can limit students. The excellent book *Boys Don't Try* (Pinkett & Roberts, 2019) holds up a mirror to some of the engrained and damaging classroom expectations about boys. For example, that they are homogeneous group, who are fundamentally different from girls or that they need to learn through competition.

Furthermore, too often a label of SEND places a ceiling on the expectations of what that young person can achieve. It comes to define who they are rather than the type of support they need.

Leading mindfully begins with self-reflection and this includes doing the uncomfortable work of reflecting on where your own assumptions and prejudices might be limiting those we are there to support. There are plenty of quality resources out there to explore individual unconscious bias, and whilst this is an important start, as leaders we also need to look at where discrepancies in expectations, or inequity in provision might be embedded in our systems.

## Inclusive Schools

What does it mean to be a deeply inclusive school? Inclusion must be baked into the culture. School must feel and be a safe space where everyone can thrive. Nowhere is this more powerful than in the classroom. In the next section, I will explore how a warm-strict culture, the classroom equivalent of 'high challenge, low threat' can be developed. This is one where high expectations are warmly and consistently communicated to students, allowing everyone feel held and valued. As explored in Section One, this is particularly beneficial for vulnerable children, as it provides opportunities for 'corrective emotional experiences' for those who might not get this same holding and modelling at home.

## Brave Schools

To lead mindfully is to be reflective and brave. We cannot shy away from expecting a lot of our children, whatever challenges they may face at home or in the wider community. We have a duty to all our students, particularly those who systemically have the odds stacked against them. We must point them warmly and firmly towards the right path and ensure they channel their rightful rage against the inequalities of our world in directions that are constructive for them.

There has been a lot of furore about exclusions in recent times. Whilst no one ever wants to exclude a child, we have to remember that exclusions are the symptom of a problem and the problem does not go away by lowering expectations or moving a child around a system. Particularly when our black, traveller and SEND communities are so disgustingly overrepresented in exclusions – which indeed they are across a range of negative outcomes measures – we must work diligently to root out racism and other forms of prejudice where they exist in our systems. This involves looking at our expectations, our curriculum, our behaviour management systems and the families and students that get the most of our time. Nonetheless, we cannot avoid putting down boundaries or lower our expectations when things go wrong. We must not be consumed by fear of being called racist and get caught bigotry of low expectations. This does a huge disservice to students by placing white fragility, instead of their needs, at the centre of our work. However, we should always listen to and reflect on the messages coming from our students and communities. Our communities are more 'woke' than ever; that is a good thing if we are prepared to get alongside it.

## The Paradox of True Inclusion

Two phrases that trip out of my mouth readily as a SENDCo are that 'all teachers are teachers of SEND' and 'good teaching for SEND is simply good teaching'. This can as easily apply to any protected characteristic. Often we think we need to do – or prove that we are doing – something different for SEND pupils, Pupil Premium Students or boys (thank God we just about stopped short of thinking we needed to do different things in the classroom for BAME students too). However, if we hone our craft, break down the constitute parts of our subjects, explain and model them clearly and provide lots of opportunities for guided practice and feedback all students will benefit, but particularly the most vulnerable. This is the joyous paradox of true inclusion.

We communicate our assumptions of students in subtle but powerful ways, the 'hidden curriculum' of inclusion. Students and particularly those who, like Kai may struggle and be looking to protect themselves are very attuned to perceptions of status. Target grades, top and bottom sets and tables, differentiation by task, withdrawal groups and SEND areas, all reinforce messages that some children are cleverer than others.

Well intentioned differentiation can also reinforce this. Mary Myatt says, 'True differentiation is a paradox' (2020). Most differentiation would not show up on a lesson plan or a book look. It happens in the here and now, it is how we adjust our questions, check for understanding or remind students to recall how they tackled this last time they struggled with it. This is responsive teaching. It happens when we know our subjects and our students well. We can build this into our planning, breaking down content and anticipating misconceptions but it always needs to be in relationship to where the child is at and always with the emphasis on making the work progressively more challenging. It is an oldie but a goodie. In her (2015) blog *Red or Green Pen*, Bodil Isaksen extends the metaphor of leaning to ride a bike by comparing the merits of tricycles and stabilisers. Whilst tricycles might provide the security of feeling like you can ride, they are not in fact a bike and this is inherently limiting. Stabilisers, on the other hand, provide support to learn to ride but when the child is balanced enough can be taken off and they can ride freely. The intention is to always withdraw our support. This way of thinking needs to be built into our long-term plans. They might wobble at times and even fall off. Remember Winnicott's (2002) notion of empathically failing a child? This is part of the learning process. As leaders we need to be comfortable with the messiness of learning, rather than being the metaphorical parent who will not let go of their child's bike.

Challenge is good in the classroom, but we need to be careful not to overload our students, particularly those who might have working memory challenges due to their school or home experiences. Section Three will explore how we find this delicate balance. Leaders need to be cognisant of this when setting their expectations of the speed that content can be covered and curriculum planning needs to be done with memory in mind. The content of the curriculum also has a powerful role to play in terms of transforming society towards equality. I have argued for the possibility of a powerful knowledge-rich curriculum to promote radical inclusion by giving all students access to 'the broader picture'. That means teaching the traditional canon in conversation with what has often been left out of it: the stories and voices of women and people of colour (Reid, 2018, 2020). I have suggested that 'we must teach the facts and also how they came to be the facts' (*ibid.*). This is both the intellectually honest and the moral thing to do, and however diverse (or not) your school is, it really matters.

None of this means that everyone is always treated the same. The paradox of equality is sometimes it means treating people differently. This is a delicate 'waltz', but the best schools know how to do it. These schools combine clarity of ethos; everyone knows what is expected of them and a deep knowledge of their children and their families. They offer personalised, wrap-around support that is tailored to need and has the lightest touch possible.

## Intervention

That means we must use robust data to identify who needs intervention and then ensure that they are evidence based, happen as early and for as short a time as possible.

Having a well-qualified, Speech and Language Therapist and Counsellor work in consultative way with the inclusion team: completing assessments; advising on intervention and feeding into whole school policies is another way to both bake inclusion into your culture and save money.

The Nurture Model is another well-established approach and one I would argue is a robust spend of pupil premium and SEND funding. Too often our students that challenge us have more segregated time with less qualified staff (Webster & Blatchford, 2013, 2019). It should be a badge of honour to teach these young people. It is a real skill to make the complex content of our subject disciplines accessible to all. Leaders committed to radical inclusion, perpetuate that message by avoiding setting and where nurture groups are necessary ensuring that their 'best' subject specialists are timetabled to teach them. In a recent article for the TES, Webster (2021) argued that perhaps rather than encouraging additional adults to develop their subject knowledge, as Ofsted have recently suggested, we should empower teaching assistants to take a more active lead in classroom management. This would allow subject specialists to have more one-to-one time with the most vulnerable students.

However, as Nicole Dempsey, of Dixons Trinity rightly pointed out on Twitter, 'When are we going to stop papering the cracks and just fix the wall?' True inclusion is getting it right for all students the first time. Thus, whilst intervention may be necessary, we should never get too attached to it. Our priority needs to be ensuring that we have the right culture and strategic priorities so that all can thrive, from the beginning.

## Building a Reading Culture

The biggest leaver we can pull to improve our student's life chances, particularly the most vulnerable is to improve their literacy. Reading is at the heart of this. In every walk of life, but particularly at university level, you need to read. Building a culture of reading must be a whole school endeavour. The paradox of which is that literacy is both a predictor of success across the curriculum and that strong subject knowledge from a range of domains is needed to be a good reader. Doug Lemov explores this in his hugely influential book *Reading Reconsidered* (2016). If we teach reading skills at the expense of a broad and balanced curriculum, we will disadvantage all our readers. Prior knowledge affects comprehension. I am a very fluent reader, yet I would struggle to read a physics paper because I do not have the prerequisite conceptual understanding. Nonetheless, if we do not teach our students to read properly and support those who are not yet reading at age related expectations effectively, then we severely limit our young people's educational experience. As a result, sometimes tailored reading intervention is also necessary.

Across the Greenshaw Trust all students start their day with reading. Over time, their teachers read a range of high-quality texts to them, cover to cover. At Phoenix we had a similar model, but we also used this time as an opportunity to provide tailored interventions. This was a toss-up but a worthwhile one in my book as it meant students did not have to be withdrawn from their timetabled subjects. We provided small groups phonics for those who could not fluently or accurately decode, with English or specialist SEND teachers and small vocabulary groups, supported by a speech and language assistant for those with specific speech, language and communication needs. Crucially they still had lots of exposure to high-quality texts because as soon as they reach the point of being able to access the mainstream (assessed through a mixture of phonics testing, reading ages and teacher judgement), they would be moved out of the group. There was no languishing in intervention for terms (or years) on end.

---

**Sean Delahoy, English Director at Greenshaw Learning Trust, Explains How his Trust Puts Reading at the Heart of Its Schools**

We have a huge focus on reading within all the schools in our trust. We bookend the day with reading for all our students in years 7–10. They have tutor reading in the morning for 20–25 minutes, where their tutor reads aloud to them. Then there is DEAR (Drop Everything and Read) time at the end of the day for 20–25 minutes, where students bring their own reading and read independently for pleasure. Our students also have 20 minutes of homework, four days a week that is dedicated to reading. This works out as over an hour of reading every day.

We work hard with our librarians, without forcing students to read certain things to shape their tastes. Often their interest is piqued through the stories they hear in tutor time.

We have made the decision to prioritise reading over other activities in tutor time. Tutor time can be really effective if a tutor is great but much less effective if they are not. We decided as a trust, what better thing to do than just read? As a result, we have let go of a diluted PSHE curriculum and a lot of wasted time in the morning.

A well-put-together start to the school day makes this possible. We have roll call in all of our schools. This includes routines such as the register and uniform and behaviour checks and deals with issues of well-being. Tutors identify where students might be struggling in roll call and flag this to the head of year.

As the teacher is the strongest reader in the room, they are best placed to bring the story to life and model excellent reading. If lots of different students are reading, it starts to lose its fluency. There tends to be more focus on who is reading than what is being said. We ask our teachers to read ahead, write synonyms for more complex vocabulary and provide a short synopsis of the story to make it accessible for students.

We have put together a Greenshaw Learning Trust Canon. Every school has access to these books but can refine it for their context. We updated it this year, identifying gaps in terms of BAME and female representation and exploring how we can better tie it in with our curriculum.

If you build a really good canon that fits the context of your school, builds a love of reading, and mirrors and builds on the curriculum, this is the best PSHE curriculum available. We have had little push back on this but there have been some parents who have raised questions around roll call. Initially they asked, 'How can tutors and students build relationships if they are just reading?' However, I only see relationships blossoming through love of reading rather than it being damaged through the wasted time of a more traditional tutor programme.

My son is now in year 10 at one of our schools. He first started secondary school outside the trust. I am an English teacher, but I had a son who was reluctant reader. This was quite painful, but we moved him, and he absolutely took off in terms of his reading. My daughter is going into year 7 in September, and she is going to be part of that too. I know full well they are getting the experience of so many rich stories. This has so many benefits: it enriches conversations, enlivens minds and creates great readers.

Looking at the data from Henley Bank in Gloucester, a small school with just under 500 students, year 7 and year 8 have each read 33 books this year. In year 9 and 10, they have read 19 and 12 books respectively. This is such a rich and solid starting point for young people.

Alongside bookending the day, we have worked hard to make sure we have course readers in all of our lessons. For example, in English if they are teaching a set text like *Treasure Island*, they will have a course reader full of essays with contextual information around Stevenson's inspirations, the character of Long John Silver, etc. Other departments have started to build this in. The intention is that we are not just creating the curriculum that is designed to make students jump through hoops to get great GCSE results but one that puts reading at the centre of everything we do. This also helps to build a culture where reading is not seen as something just done in English lessons. Every departments got something to say and add to our reading culture.

We have a growing number of primary schools in the trust. We are spending time looking at our secondary curriculum to ensure it really builds on what is taught at primary. What comes across powerfully is that they are good at developing a strong foundation of knowledge about language, the nuts, bolts and grammar of language in primary. It is important that we do not lose sight of that. As students become more mature, we can build on this and unlock not just foundational knowledge of language but the how and the why. This real helps develop student's passion for reading.

To make sure we do not leave anyone behind, we use the NGRT test to determine students reading scores. In the past we have collected reading data and not done awful lot with it except set and expect teachers to differentiate. Now we make sure that we identify those that are not yet ready to access our curriculum, and we have introduced a programme of direct instruction (DI) for students with reading scores significantly lower than their chronological age. This programme substitutes the standard curriculum for 12 weeks.

People can get nervous about students missing mainstream, but if they need something to get them at the same level, it is better to have something intensive and evidence based for a short space of time that have them flounder alongside their peers for years. Before we put Shakespeare in front of them, we have to make sure that they are secondary ready.

As part of the DI programme, the students sit a test. This provides the data to work out if they need a reading or writing intervention and what specific areas (for example phonics or vocabulary) they need support with.

It is staffed by Higher Level Teaching Assistants (HLTAs). Again, some colleagues get nervous about the least-qualified teachers supporting the most vulnerable students. However, as the training is so well put together and the lessons are scripted and there are no more than 15 students per class, it does not need a qualified teacher to lead the lessons. That said, we have a very strong group of HLTAs, and we do not yet have a huge amount of data yet. It is very much infancy. However, the data that we do have is extremely positive. Intervention is such a difficult concept to get right, it can be done so badly and make very little difference except to say to external observers that 'we are providing something'. DI feels different, so watch this space.

We work really hard to make sure everyone promotes the idea that reading is part of the fabric of the school. Students know that other teachers will come in and read to them and ask them about what they are reading. This starts with SLT but then involves everyone else across the school.

In our schools, if not all teachers are 100 percent confident in delivering the programme, we make sure we provide support to get them there. This only works well if we've got the complete backing of the school leadership team. SLT have to be everywhere in morning reading. They go into as many rooms as they can. Slowly, it begins to take shape. You recognise who is struggling, or they come to you because they feel you are right beside them. We might, for example, buddy up an AHT in with one tutor to model reading for 10 minutes every day.

It is also important to make sure the CPD programme includes training on tutor-time reading. We have put together a standard operating procedure for this. It is not that we want a robotic approach, but we do not want to waste a second of the student's time. Our CPD outlines the routines and procedures before the session: teachers should read ahead and mark up the text and should have a reading ruler ready at the start of the session. When the session begins, the teacher starts with a recap; they are always the one reading, and this is always done standing up. When other adults enter the room, they pick up the reading from the tutor; all students have their books flat and track the text with rulers. Reading continues right up to the bell, and then there are exit procedures to follow. We provide a PowerPoint slide for every novel on the cannon, and every school has a Tutor Time Reading Lead who monitors the programme and delivers the CPD.

# Working with Communities and Families

Mindful leaders are not afraid to guide parents and carers when they need support but they are careful not to become paternalistic. The relationship with parents and carers should be one that is dyadic, that values families as a rich source of knowledge and support for our students. Schools committed to this work alongside parents in a range of ways, for example by ensuring homework is accessible for all or providing guidance around screen time and other concerns that school and home might share.

The provision that Reach Academy and their Children's Hub provide to the community of Feltham is explored in the below interview with Mei Lim, the Hub's director. At Reach academy, leaders conduct a home visit for every new student that comes to the school. This supports them to understand the child in their entirety and bridges the gap between home and school. In my experience home visits are invaluable for building and deepening the dyadic relationship. You learn so much about a child and investing in relationships with families pays dividends.

I have been deeply inspired by hearing Ed Vaikner (Ed to his students and their families), Co-Founder and CEO of the Reach Foundation explain the lengths they would go to support their vulnerable families, be that with immigration paperwork, finding work or childcare. In my own experience, sometimes something as simple as offering to hold the baby so Mum has a space to think whilst you talk can be unimaginably helpful. On that note, let us not call her Mum. If her names Amber, use it or even better, ask her what she would like to be called. The power of introducing yourself with your first name, or making a little small talk, recalling a detail from the past perhaps to show that you 'hold the family in mind' in breaking down barriers with families should not be underestimated.

---

**Mei Lim, Former Primary Head Teacher and Director of the Reach Children's Hub in Feltham Explains Reach's Cradle-To-Career Provision**

The Reach Children's Hub grew out of the work of Reach Academy Feltham, and together, the two organisations now provide a cradle-to-career pipeline of support for children and families in Feltham. Our founders, Ed Vainker and Rebecca Cramer, wanted to open a free school that offered something different for children and young people. Inspired by charter schools in the US and place-based initiatives such as the Harlem Children's Zone, they sought to establish a school that put relationships with children, families and the wider community at its centre so that children could flourish personally and academically.

Feltham in the west of Hounslow was identified as a community that could benefit from a new free school, for several reasons. Young people growing up in Feltham are more likely to achieve worse outcomes than their peers in other parts of the borough, across a range of indicators. There are systemic reasons for this – low rates of employment, low wages, historical underinvestment – and this has often contributed to a feeling of being 'left behind'. Even whilst there is a strong sense of identity amongst many of the community (who identify as living in Feltham, not Hounslow or even London) there is also a lack of social cohesion and many people experience social isolation. Regardless of these challenges and the barriers some people face, the community is rich with inspiring individuals, groups and organisations who share a passion for the area and a commitment to its young people, which is why it is such an exciting place to be based.

Reach Academy Feltham opened in 2012 and is an Ofsted-rated outstanding, all-through mainstream school that has been built up year on year and which now educates over 900 children aged 2–18. The vision of the school is that every child will be able to enjoy a life of choice and opportunity and the belief is that this can only be achieved by working as a team alongside parents and the wider community.

This ethos has been built into the fabric of the school in several ways. It is a small school, with only 60 children in each year group, even at secondary, which helps staff to build deep relationships with all pupils and their families. Home visits are an integral part of how we work at Reach and take place throughout the school year. Right from the start, the school employed a family support worker, whose remit is to do wider work with the family, such as modelling parenting strategies or helping families to access statutory support. What is more, everyone is called by their first name. It sounds like a small thing, but every step that removes boundaries and the traditional hierarchy or power structure that can exist between teachers and parents helps to make a difference and allows for a real sense of building a partnership and a shared understanding that we are raising children as a community.

Over the years and based on their experiences with the school and insights gathered from a local consultation, Ed and Rebecca began to develop the idea of a Children's Hub, a community resource that would enable Reach to offer cradle-to-career support from 0–21, moving beyond solely educating and supporting children from aged 2–18. What we increasingly know about a child's early brain development is that to really make a difference and ensure every child has the best start in life, we need to be offering parents perinatal support. A child's brain develops to 80% of adult size by the age of 3, and evidence shows the impact parental mental health can have on healthy brain development, even in utero. Furthermore, if parents have positive experiences of support and continuity of care from pregnancy, not only will this impact positively on the baby's healthy development, but the parents are more likely to continue to engage with ongoing support.

We also know that people do not always ask for help because it is a really difficult thing to do. However, if you can build trusting relationships through activities that people want to be a part of – a baby group or a cooking class – and by providing them with the time and space to be listened to, then gradually these parents may open up and tell you their story. And at that point you can identify any further, specialised support that they may need and, through signposting or brokering relationships, make sure they get the right help, at the right time. The importance of having a physical space where people can come should not be underestimated: it's about bringing people into a space where they can be nurtured and really listened to, where they feel a sense of belonging, where they can start to feel connected to others, have opportunities to get involved and so on, especially as the benefits to mental health and well-being that come from giving to and connecting with others are well documented.

The importance of providing continuity of care through trusting relationships and keeping people connected is also one of the reasons why we support students at the other end of the pipeline when they graduate from Reach Academy. Transition into further education, training or employment can be hard. Our vision to ensure every child and young person can enjoy a life of choice and opportunity means we have a responsibility to our students that goes beyond just supporting them to gain an apprenticeship or university place – we need to help them see it through.

In fact, although we talk about supporting children and young people aged 0–21 through our cradle-to-career model, in reality the 'career' part of it now stretches even further as we've begun to extend our offer to working with parents. The impact of financial stress and insecurity on parental mental health and the subsequent negative impact this can have on the home learning environment for children means that we focus a lot on developing parental capabilities. As the pandemic has exacerbated these stresses for many of our families, we are now offering micro-grants to help parents re-train or gain new qualifications and providing coaching and networking opportunities. We are in the process of setting up a Parent Peer Programme, which will train volunteers in peer support and group facilitation. The personal benefits of volunteering are well known but this is also about building capacity and sustainability across the system – not by growing the Hub team but by developing parent leaders, something we are also strategic about through our community organising work with Citizens UK.

This brings me onto how we actively seek to work in partnership with other organisations to affect change. We never want to duplicate services, and we're not precious about 'owning' or leading work – what matters to us is doing excellent work with excellent people and organisations to bring about excellent outcomes for children and young people. So the Hub collaborates with other charitable organisations in the area, local authority services, health and educational professionals, parents and residents, to deliver a range of services. In 2020, we decided to approach this in a more intentional way and began developing our collective impact model, inspired by Strive Together in the US and other place-based systems-change initiatives in the UK, such as North Birkenhead Cradle-to-Career (Right to Succeed). The Feltham Convening Partnership launched in September 2020 and, a year on, involves almost 50 cross-sector partners who come together and take collective action to change the system in order to improve cradle-to-career outcomes for children and young people.

Evaluating the impact of everything we do is something we take seriously, and we spend time and effort developing clear theories of change as part of this process. We only ever want to implement evidence-based interventions, such as Family Links. Where there are appropriate opportunities to innovate, we are rigorous about evaluating the impact and acting on what we learn. One of the challenges we face is how to measure not only the impact of individual interventions but the cumulative impact of someone engaging with multiple Reach Children's Hub interventions over time. To this end, one of the approaches we've used is a 'Contribution Mechanisms Analysis' in order to i) capture the contribution we can be confident we are making and ii) identify the specific mechanisms that enable this so we can do more of the good stuff whilst also acknowledging all of the other factors that will likely be contributing to positive outcomes for a person – not least the school and all the staff who may be involved with a child and their family.

It's this combined effort between the school and the Hub that really explains our cradle-to-career model. Both institutions work in very different ways, but it's the combined effort that results in sustained impact. The school's work is fast-paced and direct, and it's relatively straightforward to see the impact (e.g. a 1:1 or group literacy intervention will help a child improve their reading levels). The Hub, on the other hand, has greater capacity to work on some of the underlying, wider causes of under-attainment. That may involve supporting parents back into work, advocating around poor housing or bringing more resource into the area. The Hub's work is messy; it takes time, and the impact is not always immediate or obvious. It's no exaggeration to say that in some cases it may take a generation to bring about change, but we are positive about our ability to do this because of the transformations already emerging.

Having established our cradle-to-career model in Feltham, we are now starting to work with other schools across the country to think about their own models and what this could look like in their contexts. Context is important and we are always clear about the fact that it's the *why* not the *what* that's really important to understand. If someone just wanted to replicate our timetable of interventions, there's no guarantee it would have the desired impact, especially as our timetable is always subject to change because we constantly adapt and respond to feedback: it's about putting people before programmes! So instead we focus on sharing why we do what we do: explaining what we've learned, our asset-based approach to community development, the tools we've found useful such as community organising, why we believe early years is so fundamental and, of course, why relationships are at the heart of everything we do.

## Multi-agency Working

This focus on relationships extends to the professional networks that sit around vulnerable students like Kai. Just like in school, much of successful multi-agency working depends on the trust and relationship between the network.

The Marmott Review in 2010 set out the clear social and economic case for action across and between services, in order to create the conditions for people to 'take control of their lives' (Marmott, 2010, p. 15). However, with increased funding pressure on schools and local authorities the capacity to make this happen is limited, the reality is many schools are still operating in narrow silos (Haye, 2016). It is easy to retreat into the comfort of our professional boundaries and work to 'cover our backs', particularly where the stakes are high and the risk of getting blamed for something lies just around the corner.

A mindful approach requires being brave and doing things a bit differently. We have to be realistic about what is out there. We live in a time of austerity, the safety net and range of interventions that once existed is no longer available. Instead, we have to get comfortable with sitting with risk, to feel and name the things that are difficult and be creative in our responses. If we maintain professional kindness and keep love for our students at core of everything we do, this can be done. Partly because the felt experience of having a strong and loving team at your back provides an opportunity for the corrective emotional experiences that so many of our most vulnerable families need. Some of our colleagues need it too and so, much like with our parents, the small human touches, offering of biscuit, remembering a detail about someone's life can go a long way to making a social worker or CAMHS worker feel as though you are all on the same team.

Before doing this though, it is helpful to reflect on how this fits in with our statutory obligations around safeguarding.

## A Note on Safeguarding

A culture of noticing, listening, reflecting, where staff know their students and families well, have high expectations of, and positive relationships with them *is* a safeguarding culture. As leaders, we must work to reduce the fear that some staff have around responding to disclosures and statutory duties. This fear, leads people to cover their backs, defer responsibility and prevents thinking and working in a joined-up way. Safeguarding is everybody's business and thus should be built into the fabric of our schools. Of course, there is a role for expertise, experience and seniority in terms of holding the most challenging of cases but we must work to de-jargon, re-humanise and democratise this work as much as possible.

## Summary

- Mindful leaders are committed to placing the needs of the most **vulnerable at the heart** of what we do.

- Many **issues** young people face are **systemic** and can **accumulate** over the life course.

- **Schools** have an **important role** to play in addressing these injustices but **can also** inadvertently **make things worse**.

- **Bolt-on** provision just will not cut it.

- We need to focus **on improving the core offer**.

- Paradoxically, this has the **effect of improving provision for everyone**.

- Focusing on **literacy** and **embedding** your school **in the community** are some suggested ways of doing this.

# 8 Support Yourself

This chapter will do the following:

- Make the case for taking care of yourself as a leader
- Outline the benefits of supervision and professional learning networks

## Knowing When to Stop

The final chapter in this section emphasises the importance of external support. The ideas and tools in this book are just a jumping off point. However, by caring for yourself you put yourself in a good position to lead emotionally healthy schools. Knowing yourself means knowing your limits. At the inaugural New Voices conference in 2018, I was witness to Headteacher Karen Connolly (@blondbonce on Twitter) deliver an excellent talk about well-being. At the end she gave us a literal piece of string, as a reminder that it was up to us to decide where to cut. It could have been a gimmick, but it stayed in my pocket for a long time and was actually a tangible reminder of my own responsibility and choice in moments when it's easy to feel you *have* to keep working.

We do not have to keep working. Not only because we are no help to anyone when we are exhausted but because stopping sends a good message to our teams. As Myatt said, strong leaders 'model what they want to see: they make a point of leaving shortly after school ends, sometimes weekly, sometimes fortnightly' (2016, p. 74). When I worked in a school with a culture of paranoia, overwork and exhaustion, it sometimes felt my team could not 'see the wood for the trees'. To try and encourage work-life balance I would make it known that I left early some days by stopping off in peoples' offices and encouraging them to do the same. Importantly this was never a dismissive 'go home now'. When someone is in the middle of a truly urgent task an insensitive boss doing this can tip them over the edge. I once had a well-meaning manager rip up my to do list, trying to encourage me to work less but totally blind to that being my exhausted mind's coping strategy.

DOI: 10.4324/9781003198482-11

Nonetheless, a gentle reminder and leading by example is important. If you stay late, your team will think they have too as well. If you are not the big boss this can take some bravery on your part. There is always the fear that by doing this you will be perceived as not working hard enough. However, leading mindfully requires doing what is right not what is least scary.

Sometimes knowing when to stop means knowing when to moving on or take a break so that you can take care of your well-being and/ or be more effective elsewhere. Saying enough is enough is a courageous act and that takes inordinate amounts of leadership. Ruth Luzmore explains her journey out of headship (for the time being) and some of the things she has learnt in the interview that follows.

**Ruth Luzmore, former primary head teacher, co-author of** *Educating Tomorrow: Learning from the Post-Pandemic World* **and current PHD candidate at the University of Durham,** discusses systemic challenges, heroic notions of leadership and emotional vulnerability, building trust/school culture and prioritising her own well-being.

The reasons I chose to step back from headship are multi-faceted. I'd had five years of a horrific commute, some days spending over four hours travelling. Whilst I liked to read (or go on Twitter) on the train and the time at the beginning and end of day allowed me to have a separation (meaning I generally wouldn't work when I got home) I found it was becoming more and more difficult to get out of bed in the morning – I was tired. Running a school during Covid had been horrendous and with the commute I was running on adrenaline and needed a break. I wanted to regain some balance and restart my PHD.

I admire those heads who stay and commit to one school 'for life', but that is not how I usually work – I can get itchy feet and I'd achieved a lot in the school that I was happy with. We had a really stable, intelligent and tight-knit team. I am extremely proud of the low turnover rate we had in the school. The right people wanted to stay. We had really worked on our curriculum and it was fabulous. Of course there is always more to be done, that is the nature of the job, with the annual cycle of the school seasons and their various asks along with the more surprising events. But before Covid hit, I did feel we were getting increasingly stuck because of finances or the lack thereof. Before Covid, I was becoming increasingly focused on about how I could make things financially viable – how could I bring in the type of additional finance the school down the road (with the affluent parent body) were bringing in to keep the offer to our pupils as high as it should be. There is a cost to keeping excellent teachers, as they (rightly) become more expensive year on year, that was a nagging problem. Before Covid, we were constantly looking for ways we could save money and we hated the idea of having to cut provision to a point which would impact on the workload of staff even more.

We can shave bits off around the edges but if you cut too much you destroy the core. Ultimately it is not about money but people, having enough people to have the time and space to think about things. Trying to do it all means we are spread too thinly.

I was responsible for safeguarding. That can take up hours of your week. As the most expensive member of staff, it was probably not the most strategic use of my time to be sitting in a Child Protection meeting for three hours but we literally had no one else to do it, they were all teaching.

This increasing responsibility of 'social work' in schools is not in and of itself something that schools cannot do. We are at the heart of our communities and we see the children all the time, but we need to fund this as a protected position properly, so we can get on with the education work too.

When you're responsible for safeguarding it can be easy to be like that tough kid in the playground and just say I'm fine. But actually having a network of others in a similar role who you can talk to and who will understand was really important for me — not only to work through problems but also to reduce stress levels. This is one of the benefits of supervision.

Something seems broken in our system. I think that having come out of education and working in something unrelated, in business and academia, it is even clearer to me. There is stress in every job but there is an intensity to stress in schools. It is abnormal but people don't always realise it. Even though the pay is okay and we get the holidays, this comes at the cost of reaching half term and getting sick.

For years I didn't have the right balance of work and home. I am aware that time and again, I would choose the needs of my school community over that of my family. Three years in a row, I forgot my sister and father's birthday – they never gave me any grief about it, but I do regret that in my busy-ness, I wasn't there for family and friends. Everyone and everything came second. I know I'm not the only one who has experienced this. I have a friend who started a miscarriage the morning when Ofsted arrived, and she just 'got on with it', another one discharged themselves from hospital to make sure they were there.

I know Ofsted have improved some things, but the pressure of getting a poor Ofsted still is a powerful motivating factor. No matter what any head says publicly, we all know if your Ofsted fails, you're likely to lose your job. The shame and humiliation of publicly being judged to not be good enough is something that can really devastate a community. You are due Ofsted, then you have Ofsted, then you're due again. It is relentless. Despite best endeavours, it is not yet an improvement system but a public judgement system that can ruin communities, workplaces and lives.

In other industries there are pressures as well but there is an added moral pressure in teaching. There is a narrative that we don't get it right, we are condemning the children to a disastrous future. Schools can make a huge difference and of course we want education to be as good as it can be, but I think we need to start putting this into perspective. I've been in those meetings as a teacher where someone is saying that every minute counts in the classroom – yes, it is important not to waste it, but if we truly start believing that, no wonder we have burnout in some schools.

But pressure can be helpful. We all need to be accountable for actions and some accountability measures have certainly improved our practice but I'd like to see there be a sensible amount. Many of my head colleagues are still on their knees, dealing with Covid-19, and the accountability and 'business as usual' attitude isn't supportive right now.

A few years ago when I'd just become a Head, the responsibility hit me quite hard. I made the active decision to seek out counselling. I would highly recommend it. It gave me some remarkable insights about myself and how much I was not interested in dealing with my own problems. My therapist said to me, 'Every time you come in, you try and talk about me. You give me a compliment and make it about me. In the nicest way possible, you're not my friend. Let's talk about you.'

It was really good to have someone to be completely honest with. When it is someone you are paying, not a friend or colleague or anyone who comes with a vested interest, it can be all about you. This doesn't often happen for us as heads or as teachers, but I learnt a lot about myself and what I needed to do to keep myself steady.

I spent a good amount of my time in education on anti-anxiety medication but six weeks after leaving I'm off all of it. I increased the dosage when it came to Covid – my doctor said it was pretty normal. I don't mind talking about that. It is not because I was working in a toxic environment – quite the opposite I had the most brilliant team around me and a really supportive parent community as a head. Ultimately for me to make good decisions, and to moderate my mood I needed some medication.

I made the decision to tell my staff about this. I told them, you might see me smiling and laughing and chatting away with people like everything's okay, but I experience stress and some dark times too and I get it. This created a climate in which we could talk about things when we were struggling. There is a tendency for leaders to feel that can't show 'weakness'. Actually, I've cried in front of members of my team – mostly out of pure pride and joy in the pupils during a school concert or performance, etc., but sometimes when something was really tough. The sense of connection that this created was brilliant, it meant that they could do the same with me.

I've never had a difficulty with expressing emotions, but I do feel that anger was the one emotion that had to be taken out the building. Go for a walk. You don't want your staff or the children to see you angry because anger makes people feel on edge or even afraid and I don't think it's acceptable. In previous workplaces I have had angry managers and it was like stepping on eggshells. It is not okay to have a workplace where people feel afraid.

We've all got a lot of patience but when you're dealing with really difficult behaviour incidents with pupils and there may be a point that you choose to step out, so that you don't end up shouting or saying something you regret. Then you might need to come back and express this, saying for example, 'I had to walk away there because I felt like this . . . when that happened.'

Part of me looking after my own well-being was becoming more emotionally intelligent in this way. Having counselling and taking anti-anxiety medication or taking time out from school leadership are not a sign of my not being able to cope. I think perhaps I will be back one day, but right now, I need a bit of a sabbatical, so I'm really able to give it all to a community. That is self-leadership and good modelling.

We all need certain things to flourish. For me that is making sure that when I got home, I did not do my school work and that I created space to engage with other interests. For some teachers the job is everything. Many colleagues are unnecessarily burning themselves out by trying to make everything perfect, every day. Rather than working late into the night they would probably do better going to a quiz night, doing something fun, to help them switch off so the pressure doesn't become all consuming.

People actively having conversations about interests outside work can gel teams together and build better teachers in the long run. They can bring that passion in in loads of ways with colleagues or students. Our staff loved a good trip to the pub and some competitive board games.

Projects like New Voices (which I co-founded with Jane Manzone @HeyMissSmith) have also given me a sense of the breadth of experiences of others in education. Schools should not be silos. I like seeing what's out there and what we can learn. I was very lucky in that my Governors gave me the flexibility to undertake my PHD whilst working. Engaging with academia keeps it a really interesting job and allows you to see things from the outside, making you better at it too.

I undertook my MA because I was interested in it rather than as career move. Through it, I discovered so much about professional development but that was a personal choice. What does that mean for a new head? There is no statutory qualification and no agreed baseline level of knowledge but there is so much understanding of finance, HR, exclusions and safeguarding that Heads need to have, not to mention the core business of developing teachers. We rely so heavily on The Key, particularly to work out what's statutory and non-statutory, it doesn't seem right.

My research has led me to explore how we build cultures of professional development. It is in all those bits that are not planned for. We can have the best training scheme in the world but it is what we do in a daily basis that really matters. How I develop my staff is the most important aspect. A lot of it is about creating communities of trust. We get there by being willing to get things wrong and say I don't know; how can we learn from this?

I don't know what my long-term plan is. I may be earning a ninth of what I was, but the simplicity is bringing me happiness. We all come to teaching because of our values, it is a great way to change the world in little ways but we don't owe anything, it is still just a job. My hope is that by finding some balance and creating the time and space for me, I will also be able to work out what it is that bothers me about the school system and find ways to address it.

# Supervision

It can be exceptionally lonely at the top. In my darkest hours, having supervision with an experienced psychiatrist was a lifeline. It offered a level of space and psychic protection, which allowed me to make sure, despite the pressure on me that I could make clear decisions and that I was able to open that metaphorical umbrella over my team and the students. And it kept me sane and helped me navigate to a space that was healthier for me and where I could have more of an impact.

Whilst it is taken as a given that those working in mental health and social work will have access to supervision, education has been slow on the uptake. Ofsted suggest that 'staff and other adults receive regular supervision and support if they are working directly and regularly with children and learners whose safety and welfare are at risk' (Ofsted, 2019a) but in many schools this is not the reality.

However, it is starting to gain traction. A recent study through Leeds Beckett University (Lawrence, 2020), has highlighted the importance of supervision for those in safeguarding roles. It has been long been argued that this should be part of the SENDCo entitlement too. Our school leaders are on the front line of this, our most precious resources. They have the biggest impact, they are paid the most and they take the fall if things go wrong. Thus, they need to be invested in. The following interview with Claire Short explains a little more about how this can work.

---

**Dr Clare Short, Consultant Child and Adolescent Psychiatrist and CEO of OpenMind. Ed Charity, Explains the Role of Supervision in Supporting School Leaders**

Supervision can be different things to different people, but it is important to state that it is not therapy. Though a supervisor might offer some guidance, it is not about being told what to do either. It offers a safe space, to pause and reflect on the day-to-day experiences of work. Particularly, those parts that are challenging, problematic or uncertain.

Trainees in psychiatry often ask me, how can I be the best. I say, 'Physician know thyself'. Knowing yourself as well as you can, as a leader, is your best starting point.

If you come into leadership with a sensitivity about how others perceive you then you are vulnerable and less likely to be a good leader. On the other hand, if you are insensitive to your relationships and how you are perceived by your colleagues, this is equally as problematic. Finding that middle ground, where you know what you bring into your leadership and are open to exploring what you don't know or might need to be attentive too is what is important.

Supervision helps people discover those parts of themselves that they are less familiar with or less attentive to. It allows us to fine tune peoples practice, in subtle but powerful ways.

Rarely do leaders give themselves this kind of space. They feel they are too busy or that they are there to look after others. Nothing could be further from the truth.

Leaders under pressure usually speed up, supervision is about slowing down. We notice things we would not see if we were going fast. This empowers us to deal with the complexity of school life, where there are no easy answers and often no answers at all.

Much of leadership is about containing. We should not underestimate this process. It's a bit like going to a child and saying, 'Mummy's here. Everything will be fine. I can see you're anxious or worried, but it's okay.' If we can contain people's expectations, anxieties and projections, without any reactivity, then people feel held. This allows them to have confidence. When people are anxious or fearful, they cannot tap into their strengths.

My experience of colleagues working in education is that they are highly skilled and have an enormous amount of day-to-day experience. It can be quite easy to lose sight of this when we are caught up responding to a crisis. What is more there may not be adequate support outside school environment. Schools often end up holding more than they set out to.

In any other services that are supporting young people and families they all have supervision. Whilst sometimes this is with line managers – which is questionable – the term and need for it is recognised. In schools this not the case, but I think it is going to change. In a way that is why I wanted to set up the charity. I saw so many good staff feeling like they were drowning but it was not them that were drowning, the system was not creating any buoyancy.

If supervision is going to be successful, it is essential that the senior leadership team and line managers of the supervisees buy it to it. Sometimes people want it for everyone else but not for themselves. I think that can be quite difficult. It suggests that their role is only looking after others, that they don't matter or influence things, but of course they do.

There needs to be a clear understanding of what supervision is and is not so there is a coherence amongst everyone. It is important decide if you want to explore your own experiences in the work environment or students and their mental health. You may not wish to just explore cases, unpicking what happened and what needs to be done next, but also what the cases induced in you. That is how it feels and the patterns that play out in your responses. It needs to be clear at the beginning because different supervisors can offer different things. Some people can provide both together and that can really work, but it is not for everyone.

The thing is to make sure that the supervisees feel they've got the right person. One size doesn't fit all. It is a sensitive issue; it is not easy to tell a supervisor that they are not the right person. So, a supervisor must be really sensitive. A good way is to ease into it is to try three sessions and then review it. This way you can assess whether it is what everyone is looking for.

There are several initiatives supported by the government, including The Anna Freud Centre, which are a good point of call. There are also lots of local services. Word of mouth. bottom-up type approaches often make the most difference. You could approach your local CAMHS service for advice, or individuals who you meet along the way that you think might be suitable. There are also clinical psychologists and therapists working in the private sector that can provide this support. Since Covid everyone is online, which makes it much easier.

Psychiatrist, psychologists and psychotherapists have differing training, but the person is the biggest variable. In general, psychiatrists might be more useful when looking at young people and families with more complex needs. For example, where there are significant concerns about mental illness. Ideally a psychologist or a psychotherapist would be focused on children. Psychologists usually explore the relationship between cognition, emotion and behaviour. There interventions are generally more structured, using CBT and its extensions. Psychotherapy has a focus on the individual and is more intensive and longer term. Drawing from sociodynamics, psychotherapists tap into significant relationships in early years. In theory psychiatrists can provide all of this, as they have multiple strands to their training. They are also able to make diagnosis and understand different types of treatment, including medication and provided they have mental health officer status they have the power to detain people. However, they may not all have the capacity to offer supervision. In the end, it is but helpful to know where the training comes from, but relationships and experience are what is key.

More information about supervision and reflective practice offered by OpenMind.Ed can be found at www.openmindedcharity.org/

## Learning and Networks

Professional support does not have to be therapeutic or reflective in nature. As Siegal's (2012) Healthy Mind Platter highlights, learning is crucial to good health. This can happen through formal or more informal channels. Twitter (despite its polarising nature) is a fabulous resource that can prompt reflection, introduce research in an accessible way to a wide audience and remind you that there are likeminded people out there, if your own school has got a bit overwhelming. New learning can breathe purpose in your work. I can make your job easier and more meaningful. However, it is a balance. The temptation can be to take on too many things at once or want to implement lots of shiny new initiatives that you hear about without a coherent plan. Remember the mantra: do a few things, really well. But also that it is for the children, not so you can Tweet about it later.

## Decompression

To achieve this, you need room to breathe. Scheduling pauses is a good idea, even if you do not think you will need them at the time, we are not robots and all need time to decompress and be ourselves. We also need to allow for things going wrong or take longer as they inevitably do. Ask yourself how am I building space into my day, week and year for this? Then give yourself permission to enjoy the calm.

## Summary

- We must make the **decision** to **support ourselves**.

- This is as important for our teams as it is our own well-being.

- **Supervision** is an excellent resource for this.

- Other forms of **professional learning** and **networks** can also support and enliven you; just be **careful not to overcommit**.

# SECTION THREE
## Leading in the Classroom

# 9 A Mindful Classroom

This chapter will do the following:

- Draw on established research to outline some suggested priorities for a calm and effective classroom
- Explain with examples what these might look like in practice

## Cognitive Load Theory

To create a classroom that is mindful, we need to take the time to stop and reflect on what is going to have the highest impact. To do this well, requires engaging with research and in reflection then, putting what we know works front and centre and streamlining everything else. Cognitive Load Theory (CLT) can support us to do this. CLT reminds us to think about attention and memory. The corollary of this is that we must attend to the content and sequencing of our curriculum. This means identifying and being explicit in our expositions about key concepts and their links and providing plenty of opportunities for recall and practice.

## Routines and Principals

If we are going to give time and attention to teacher explanations, then we do not want to busy our classrooms with too many distractions or waste learning time managing poor behaviour. Instead, we must put our energy into doing a few things, that we know work, well.

When implemented with love and strong subject knowledge, high impact routines or teacher habits have a powerful role to play. Rosenshine's principles[1] and many of the routines set out in Lemov's (2014) *Teach Like a Champion* (*TLAC*) provide a helpful framework for making decisions around what might be prioritised for classroom practice. These are certainly not new ideas, nor are they are the only approaches that will have an impact. Many more eminent than me, have written on this topic. In Chapter 6 John Kirkman talks eloquently about how they developed their principles of teaching at Mossbourne Victoria Park and *Rosenshine's Principles* are explored in forensic depth in Tom Sherrington's book *Rosenshine's Principle's in* Action (2019) if you wish to understand them further.

One way to reduce the cognitive load is to do the same things, that we know work, every lesson so that they become habitual. When these things are second nature to you and the children, the classroom becomes a safe and predictable base and you can be present and responsive to their needs. When done right they free teachers up to be in the now in their classroom. That means they can focus on what the children are doing, saying and thinking, rather than being distracted by their own performance or trying to distract them with busy activities. This notion of truly being present in the classroom will be explored further in the next (and final) chapter.

Routines applied consistently across a school can be transformative. However, you cannot *TLAC* your way to excellence. Routines must be underpinned by strong subject knowledge, carefully thought through curriculum and resources and a strong and consistent behaviour system. This chapter will walk through my suggestions for the pedagogical priorities of a mindful classroom but this section cannot happen without the whole school priorities, set out in Section Two, first being in place.

## Lesson Beginnings

When students step into your classroom, they need to feel that they belong and that you are in charge. Greeting each student by name at the door has numerous benefits. It allows you to have individual interactions with each student and to build relationships. It enables you to set the tone of the lesson and troubleshoot any problems to ensure that, when they cross the threshold, your students are ready for learning. Conveying calm and warmth through your words, tone and body language is key in developing this routine successfully.

*Teach like a Champion* (TLAC) helpfully breaks down this technique (#41), 'Threshold', into its constituent parts. It suggests having one foot in the classroom and one in the corridor, to allow you to see what is going on in both spaces. The technique Strong Voice (#56) provides the instruction to 'Square up, Stand Still' (Lemov, 2014, p. 414). This unknowingly seems to me to be polyvagal informed. By having two feet on the floor, slightly wider than your hips. you feel and appear grounded and secure in yourself. What has come to be called 'Power Posing' (Cuddy, 2012). Keeping neutral body language that is limited in movement along the midline is key to communicating that you are both calm and centred.

Recall the exercise in Chapter 2: acknowledge; pause; release; centre, combining this with threshold is a way to prepare yourself to step into your classroom with authority. This will be explored further in the next chapter. My expectation has always been when they step over my threshold, there is silence. To do this I must be clear with the students: 'in our classroom, we. . .' and ready to calmly, hold that line.

# Review of Previous Learning

The first thing students do when they come into the room is complete an independent 'Do Now' task, a short (five question) multiple choice retrieval quiz. The format is the same every lesson. This reduces the cognitive load and the amount of disruption as, once it is embedded, students never have to ask what to do (more about this in the next chapter).

Starting the lesson with a predictable retrieval practice task, serves many purposes. It is a settler, it builds independence, it allows you to manage your threshold and take the register without the students expecting any input from you. There is a wealth of evidence from Cognitive Science that repeated, low stakes testing, consolidates information from working memory into long term memory (Brown, Roediger, & McDaniel, 2014). This is particularly effective if the retrieval is spaced out, meaning that concepts from prior learning are retested at different intervals.

Retrieval practice also serves to add narrative and coherence to your curriculum by making conceptual links explicit. For example, in Religious Studies the concept of sacrifice could be explored in early animist traditions in at the beginning of Year 7, then relooked at in Judaism towards the end of the year and then returned to in Year 8 in relation to the crucifixion of Jesus in Christianity. Over time this builds students schema, their mental models of our disciplines, moving them from a simplistic understanding to a rich recognition of the nuances of the category.

Situating the learning of an individual lesson within a context that students are already familiar with, makes the purpose of the learning relevant to students and answers that perennial question of 'why do I need to know this, Miss?'. The individual learning has meaning in relation to the curriculum as a whole. In my experience, students really love seeing ideas that they recognise come up time and time again, this builds their confidence and gives a sense of meaning and purpose to the subject. If these links can also be built across subject disciplines, even better. Whilst at John Madjeski Academy in Reading, I developed a coherent humanities curriculum that was explicit about the links between History, Geography and RE (Reid, 2018). There is great potential for this to be done across a range of subjects, if time is set aside for subject leads to co-plan.

Retrieval tasks should be quick to do and even quicker to mark. Build in a routine of Cold Call (#31), (Lemov, 2014, pp. 249–262) where teachers target questions rather than taking hands up to ensure everyone participates. Not only does it build rigour and participation, but it allows you to get a sample of what students do and do not know. Just make sure you ask the question before calling the students name to keep everyone thinking about the answer.

Students should mark and annotate answers where there are mistakes, or something is missing. This is a live activity, rather than a procedure to get through. This means that the information gathered in should be used to tailor your lesson. Pause and reteach if necessary. There is enough time! There is no point racing through a curriculum that students have not fully understood.

It is important to provide students with a chance for success in their first question, particularly for students with low self-esteem as learners. So, start easy and get progressively more difficult. This increase in challenge can also occur over a lesson sequence. For example, the first retrieval activity could be asking students to match new vocabulary to its definition, then in the next lesson they might be asked to choose the correct definition from a choice of three (including two plausible distractors). Next, they could be only given the definition and must recall the word it relates to and then might be given the word but must write the definition. Finally, they must explain it in their own words.

Starting your lesson in this way ensures homework is meaningful and equitable. You can set students the task of consolidating the information at home, in the knowledge that they are going to be tested on it in the next lesson. This task should not require any adult input. This is because we know that many of the most vulnerable students often do not have regular access to this. The independence also builds good revision habits, so these are not something that needs to be frantically taught in the run up to exams.

Low-stakes quizzing helps us move beyond dichotomous thinking about testing. There is an assumption, amongst some with a progressive bent, that testing is bad for kids. Whilst it is true that many schools have become like 'exam factories', teaching too much to the test at the expense of a broad and balanced curriculum and that adult anxiety about results is often passed to students. However, when done right, testing has an important role to play in moving information from short term to long term memory. What is more, it is also satisfying for students, as they get to see the progress that they are making in real time. To do this, testing should be low stakes and routine. There should be no whiff of competition or threat of humiliation if they do not know the answer.

## Square Up, Stand Still

When you are ready to start delivering new content, take another moment to acknowledge, pause, release and centre (see Chapter 3 for a reminder). Choose a spot at the front of your classroom where you are visible to the whole class, what is referred to in *TLAC* as the pastor's perch. Return to this spot and 'be seen looking' whenever you want to gather your student's attention. Once established, this subtle non-verbal technique cultivates a huge amount of presence in the classroom.

## Exposition

When your students are ready to listen, smile and begin your explanation. Well-prepared explanations using the technique 'economy of language' (Lemov, 2014, p. 414) and few words combined with deliberate use of tone and gesture will convey your point and passion for the subject. Fiercely defend everyone's right to have access to this by insisting that students are silent and sitting up straight when you (or anyone else) is talking to the class. Encourage students towards the right behaviours by 'narrating the positive' (for example, 'Thank you Jamila for sitting up straight and demonstrating excellent active listening').

## Scaffolding

Keeping the capacity of working memory in mind, it is important to present new information in small steps. Giving time over to scripting explanations can help us unbundle our thinking and make our explanations really clear and logical. Dual coding (for example, projecting some simple graphics or doing an illustration under the visualiser) can be used to support this exposition and make the ideas that we want to get across stick in our students' memory.

There should be a desirable level of difficulty in the subject matter itself. This needs to be carefully scaffolded so all students can access it. This scaffolding should be built into long-, medium- and short-term planning as it is intrinsically tied to the curriculum content. These plans should also indicate how support is gradually taken away so that the difficulty level continues to increase.

## Modelling

Another of Rosenshine's findings, which is highly relevant to a streamlined class-room, is the importance of modelling. Much of the need to give feedback can be stripped back if things are modelled well in the first place.

A visualiser is an excellent tool for supporting students to engage with the texts or resources of your subject community. It offers an opportunity to model good scholarship in terms of how you engage with these resources, making explicit reading, thinking and annotating processes. Close readings and subject-specific techniques can also be modelled. A helpful idea is to keep a model exercise book. This allows you to demonstrate exactly what you are looking for and is an excellent resource to help students catch up if they miss lessons.

The intention of modelling is to slowly transfer ownership to students: 'I do, we do, you do'. There are many different approaches to modelling, with some that will work better in your subject that others. Worked examples, where the teacher demonstrates then supports students to independent work through guided practice, work well in technical subjects, whereas joint construction, where student and teachers co-construct an answer or piece of writing favour literacy-based lessons. Unpicking prepared model answers helps to set a standard to attain to, whilst live modelling can be helpful for modelling thinking in real time and making it seem attainable. Student models are also useful for this. Sometimes a poor example can be helpful in demonstrating common errors or misconceptions too. These are often engaging for students, who tend to quite like catching you out.

The visualiser is an incredible tool for giving feedback too. Show call, *TLAC* technique #39, is a visual version of cold call where you pick student work and analyse it under the visualiser (Lemov, 2014, pp. 289–298). It can be a fantastic opportunity to both build a culture of celebration of good work and demystifying the feedback process by unpicking the strengths and weaknesses of a piece of work. However, if not handled right, it can make students nervous, and as with anything, it is all about the culture of your classroom and *how* it is implemented. Show call should be normalised, low stakes and celebratory. It is helpful to have a 'roll-out speech' to explain your rationale to students before building it into your routine over time.

## Challenge and Questioning

This environment, of high expectations for all and careful scaffolding and modelling, facilitates radical inclusion. No matter a child's starting point or challenges, high academic and relational standards are expected. An ethos of 'Everyone participates' is lived and breathed.

Cold call combined with no opt out (#11), where students are supported to find the right answer rather than saying 'I don't know' reinforces this (*ibid* pp. 90–92). As with any challenge, it must be accessible and well handled. Where students have additional needs, language barriers or confidence issues, this must be responded to sensitively, discretely and warmly.

I have written before about where I went wrong in cold calling in my early career (Reid, 2020). Cold call should appear random, but students should not feel that you are trying to catch them out. They should instead feel a healthy amount of challenge that spurs them on to 100% participation.

It is useful to have a 'roll-out speech' for your questioning techniques – cold call and no opt out – so they never feel anxiety inducing or personal but still ensure that all students are held accountable. When you are able to combine strong subject knowledge and knowledge of your students, this becomes easy.to do. It is important to think carefully about your questions and the answers you are looking for. Your students should never have to play 'Guess what is in my head'. By unbundling your questions into their constituent parts, you can then target them at the students you want to check have a grasp of that particular piece of information.

## Pause Points

One of the most helpful things to come out of the pandemic were the myths that remote learning exposed, that we could just make a PowerPoint and think it was a lesson or, worse, instruct the children to google it. Many a computer-room-based 'research' lesson had already taught me that this was nonsense, but now the importance of the teacher, particularly for the most disadvantaged, has been made explicitly clear. What is more, online teaching has forced teachers to hone their skills, and Uncommon Schools' Principles of Remote Teaching have helped to codify this.

To facilitate slow and responsive teaching a particularly helpful technique is pause points. In the context of online learning, these are intended to be points in a lesson that students would pause the video and reflect. However, transposed to a live classroom environment, they do wonders for not only ensuring an exposition is coherent and understood but also helping bring you back into the room. That is to remind you to check in with your students where you might have got a bit caught up in your own explanation.

A focus on pause points not only transforms the classroom experience; it also impacts planning. It has required me to be even more granular about the content and sequencing of my explanations.

The idea is that, during an exposition (ideally supported by use of a visual-iser), you pepper your explanation with immediate questions that check students' understanding of what you just told them. Not only does this maintain students focus and check their understanding, but it also slows your lesson right down. Claire Couves explains how in the following interview.

---

### Claire Couves, Assistant Head Teacher for Teaching and Learning at Reach Academy Feltham

The work we did on pause points came from our reflections during in the lockdown. When we watched our expositions online, we realised that teachers speak really fast. On the other end of the computer, students could not keep up with the speed and compre-hend in a really clear way. As a result, we introduced the idea of pause points. These were points where teachers asked students to pause the video and do x. This helped them to maintain attention throughout which we know is fundamental to their learning.

When we came back to school, we realised this is as true in the classroom as it is online. The speed with which teachers talk makes it easy for children to get lost. We want our expositions to be clear if students are to encode new information into their schemas. To do this we need to slow down.

This is quite a tough call for a teacher as it means covering less. We have to make decisions about what we want to cover well rather doing all the things superficially.

Everything that we do in terms of teaching and learning at Reach leads into that. Our handbook is focused on the habits that lead to effective learning. When we decided what to include, we also had to decide what not to do. In terms of leadership, deciding what not to do is as important (and harder) than deciding what to do. You need to be clear on priorities for your context. We know that our students have gaps in their learning, and thus, efficient methods for transferring knowledge are important in our context.

Pause points require students attention. They allow you to manage the impartation of new information in a way that supports retrieval. When students are able to remember more, this actively builds their schema. It also reminds you, as the teacher, to be really present. By pausing, checking the room, scanning, not only am I calmer, but I can also be more sure of what my students have understood. Over time this leads to a much deeper understanding.

It can be effective to vary pause points. We have talked a lot about using 'cold call' – that is, posing a question verbally – but you can also use 'choral response' or 'everybody writes'. Have variety in your exposition. They serve different purposes. Call and response is useful for short answers and recalling prior knowledge. Cold call is helpful for practicing new knowledge. Everybody Writes builds a depth of understanding and prepares students for independent practice.

This preparation makes the students really feel safe to tackle independent writing tasks. We know that feeling safe in school is intimately linked to being successful. By constantly providing these opportunities for students to get the questions right and narrating their success, you are able to build their confidence with new knowledge, particularly if you combine this with thinking time. Pose a question, pause, then ask a child's name (so that they have time to get to the answer before you call on them). If you are too fast, this is instantly stressful. By building the feeling of success, you create an illusion of pace when in fact the actual pace is slowed down. This leads to a much deeper learning experience.

## Streamlined Assessment

Effective assessment is streamlined – that is, it is manageable and meaningful. It can be helpful to have more extended pause points, where you get a more comprehensive over view of how much students have grasped your exposition, what is sometimes referred to as hinge questions. I like to come up with some statements about the lesson. This should include some plausible distractors. I then ask students to use their fingers to indicate which statements are true (Figure 9.1).

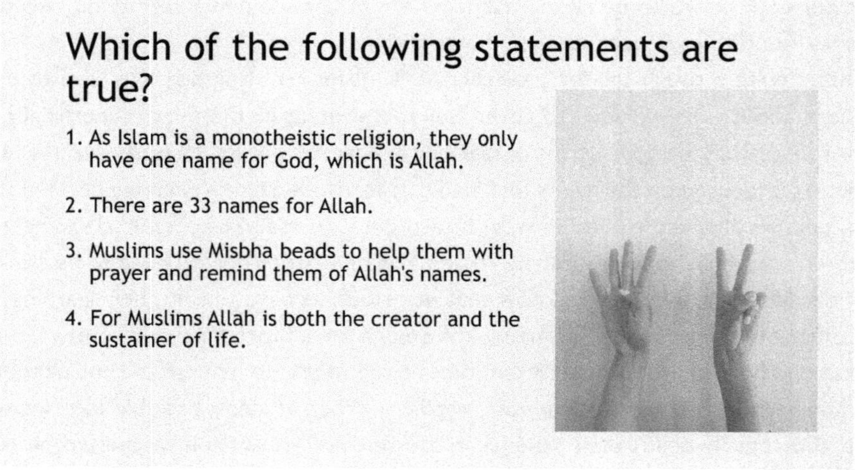

## Which of the following statements are true?

1. As Islam is a monotheistic religion, they only have one name for God, which is Allah.

2. There are 33 names for Allah.

3. Muslims use Misbha beads to help them with prayer and remind them of Allah's names.

4. For Muslims Allah is both the creator and the sustainer of life.

**Figure 9.1** Example of quick in-class assessment to address misconceptions

You can see this at a glance and then you can assess whether anything needs to be retaught or students are ready to work independently.

## Listening

It is important to really listen to the answers our students give, rather than becoming too focused on our own questioning. We need to expect high quality responses. These should come in full sentences and students should be (gently) corrected or asked to rephrase their answer until they get it right. Sometimes responses to questions need to be scaffolded. If we are aiming for a high level of discourse, where students are doing a higher ratio of work than the teacher, students need encouragement to build on and challenge each other's answers in a constructive way. This can be scaffolded through sentence stems. Displaying examples like 'I maintain that. . .', 'I see it differently because. . .' or 'Despite disagreeing on. . .' somewhere visible until they become second nature for students is a useful way to do this.

Most importantly, when we listen to these answers, we get a window into what our students do and do not understand. We need to respond to this data in a meaningful way, changing our lesson if need be, not rigidly sticking to your plan. More on this in the next chapter.

Do not be disappointed if students do not know the answer, you have just been given important information to help you do your job, it might indicate that you are challenging them which is a good thing, or you might have assumed prior knowledge that they do not have, or they may have not been listening. Either way, as long as you do something to adjust your teaching to respond to it, it is an opportunity to enrich the students learning experience. It is also an opportunity to model a learning mindset to the students. An excellent example of this came from @VallanceTeach on Twitter, who described a colleague saying to a student, 'I'm really glad you made that mistake because it allowed us to see that.'

This approach has the power to be revolutionary for student's sense of self-esteem as a learner and beyond. Responsive teaching, when done well is so energising for students, it allows them to truly track their progress. This was always the promise of AfL. However, even in its rebranded form, responsive teaching can very quickly become a distortion, if the focus is anything other than learning for learning's sake. The stress of TAGS and CAGs that the pandemic brought aside, I believe there is real possibility for us to reclaim assessment in a way that is meaningful and positive for our students.

To do this, though, requires us to attend to our own stress. If we feel under pressure around assessment, this will invariably filter down to our students. It is important that we resist a high-stakes approach (for example, not putting children in detention if they do not reach a high enough score in a test). That is not to say that we cannot convey the importance of homework in other ways or insist any students that are struggling to come to a supportive catch-up session to help them with revision. However, none of this should be couched in the language of punishment.

## Guide Student Practice

The temptation can be to try and pack too much content into our curriculum or sequence of lessons. We need to allow plenty of time for consolidation and independent practice so students can engage with what they learn on their own terms. This may not happen every lesson; you may front load teacher-led learning and then have stretches of independent working time.

This time is golden and should be silent. Particularly when we are nervous, we often want to narrate everything or buzz manically about responding to student questions. However, having checked with a sample of students that they understand the task, a mindful teacher pauses and watches their class before, pen in hand, taking a carefully thought through route around the class. When they do this, they pause to read student work, sometimes asking quiet questions but often just putting a dot in the margin to indicate to students where they want them to improve their work.

## Feedback

Feedback has become confused with marking, something we need to demonstrate that we are giving at allotted times according to a policy, rather than a fundamental element of classroom practice. The best feedback is responsive and in the moment. This is the kind that happens when, on your rounds, you notice a common error or shared misconception, and you stop the class to point it out. Sometimes this is doable within the lesson alone. Other times, it may require going over in a whole new lesson or set of lessons.

Carefully reading students' work as you circulate the room during and after the lesson offers lots of information. Rather than spending hours writing personalised comments, the common themes can become part of whole class feedback. When used to inform the planning process, it gives you a chance to really model and explain what you want to see from the students rather than expecting them to figure it out from your scrawled handwriting.

Either way, marking should inform you planning and make the students work harder than you. Whole-class feedback, in the following illustration, is another way of doing this. Often students do not know what to do with your feedback, so going through it under the visualiser and breaking it down explicitly can really help to clarify this process (Figure 9.2).

| Successes | | Next | |
|---|---|---|---|
| | | | |
| SPAG | Presentation | Unfinished Tasks | Other |

**Figure 9.2** Example of whole-class feedback sheet

## Summary

- Taking time to **reflect** and **engage with research** helps you focus on the things that will really make a difference in the classroom.

- **Rosenshine's principles** take into account **cognitive load theory** and are a helpful **framework** for a **streamlined classroom**. Simplified, these are retrieval practice, chunking new information through careful sequencing, providing models, regular questioning, opportunities for guided and independent practice and plenty of feedback.

## Note

1 www.aft.org/sites/default/files/periodicals/Rosenshine.pdf.

# 10    The Mindful Teacher

This chapter will do the following:

- Explore the importance of healthy adult authority and being present in the classroom

- Consider how this might be 'embodied'

- Suggest some ways we can support students to be more present and reflective

Professional development, systems, techniques, routines, and planning are all tools to support teaching, but they are not the teaching in itself. The raw human act of showing up for your students, relating to them, sharing your knowledge, questioning, listening to their answers and responding is teaching. If we are too caught up in our own performance, then we cannot really be present, and as such, we will never reap the rewards that our profession can offer. Yet there is a balance because the better you plan, the more able you are to be responsive and in your authority in the classroom.

## Healthy Adult Authority

What happens in class does not occur in a vacuum. The ethos in the classroom flows from the ethos in the school. The emotional space that the teacher is in, how regulated or dysregulated they are, will have an impact on their students. As Paul Dix is fond of saying, 'You make the weather' (2017, p. 89). If we come into the classroom relaxed and centred, we stand a better chance of having a calm and orderly lesson than if we tear from a meeting, slightly irritated or overwhelmed.

There is a nuance to this, which, in a culture that so often reads things as binary, I think it is important to emphasise. As teachers we are not responsible for, nor can we fix, all of society's ills. It is imperative that we do not take on too much. I know that I have been guilty of identifying with heroic leadership notions in the past. Not only is this unsustainable, but by taking too much responsibility for students'

                    DOI: 10.4324/9781003198482-14

behaviour in the classroom, it deprives them of the opportunity to develop resilience and independence.

True authority comes from having a level of certainty and emotional security yourself. A healthy adult is present and attuned to their own needs and those of others. As a result of this, they notice what is needed and know how to provide and hold appropriate boundaries.

## Boundaries

We need to be explicit about what we expect of our students and what will happen when those expectations are not met. All students benefit from clear and warmly held boundaries but particularly those with insecure attachment, for whom the world is a scary or unpredictable place. With our certainty, we can be what Winnicott refers to as a 'container' for others (2002).

We must let children learn to regulate themselves, that *empathic failure* that Winnicott (2002) also refers to. Sometimes this comes both from modelling and explaining what you want to see and sometimes by letting young people make mistakes and face the consequences of their actions. If this is done with love and there are options for repair, then having boundaries in this way is nothing to be afraid of.

This form of authority makes children feel safe. If the teacher is not really in charge, a hidden curriculum, often shaped by peer hierarchies, emerges that children must then navigate (Bennett, 2020). This is unhealthy for any child, particularly the more vulnerable ones. Clear structures, where pupils know how things work, provide a secure base. This breeds positive relationships and healthy curiosity. This is not to imply that students cannot make good decisions and lead others, but it must be built up gradually and needs to be rooted in adult authority.

## Hold Yourself

If we recall what we have learnt about how the brain operates under stress, we are reminded that stress is a fundamentally embodied process. Therefore, truly being in our authority (or being the adult) is not something we can just 'think our way into, we also have to embody it'.

To be in healthy adult authority involves being both consistent and congruent. Congruency is a kind of internal consistency. It comes from being present in the classroom and aligning your internal experience with your body language, your words and your actions. Consistency comes from embodying this writ large. Over time, doing what you say you will makes you emotionally predictable, safe. This is really hard to do, it is tough be the adult all the time and particularly in moments of crisis.

To get to this place of congruency, we as adults need to be safe and supported. We need to be held by the culture of our schools, those above us, and be able to hold ourselves. The tools in Section One and Two are there to support you to develop the wider school culture and the personal awareness and regulation to do this. The previous chapter has explored what some of the priorities and routines in a mindful classroom might be. These are not meant to be a straitjacket but a helpful framework. We cannot do everything, so having some guiding principles helps us feel clearer and safe. By doing a few things well, your cognitive load in the classroom (both for teachers and students) is significantly reduced. This chapter will explore the more intangible parts of this persona: how you hold yourself, your body language, tone and ability to handle things when they get difficult. Whilst there are no quick fixes, there are ways to help you to exude a sense of calm, clarity and warmth even when you do not yet fully feel it.

## Warm Strict

In *Teach Like A Champion*, Lemov offers a helpful starting point for this, He suggests that as a teacher, 'you should be caring, funny, warm, concerned, and nurturing – but also strict, by the book, relentless, and sometimes inflexible' (2014, p. 348). You narrate your decision-making process to the children: 'Because I care about you, there are consequences.' You recognise your responsibility to decide and hold the boundaries. This cannot be delegated to the children.

Being consistent in this way does not mean you are required to be monotonous or rigid. Quite the opposite, a warm-strict approach is playful and responsive. It models appropriate emotional responses: you are shocked when things are shocking, firm when things are not okay and delighted when things go well, all the time holding your students with unconditional positive regard.

## Responsive

Attuned consistency is also responsive to the needs and age of the group. Our expectations, routines and boundaries will change as our students become older. It requires some discernment to know when to hold the line and when to maintain the principles established but loosen the edges a little.

Much like with scaffolding, where the aim is always to get rid of it and build more independence, you should work towards establishing a professional adult relationship (by the end of sixth form). Start with the stabilisers firmly on; it is always easier to take them off than it is to try and fit them when you are riding around chaotically.

From a place of adult authority, you can explain, model and scaffold appropriate behaviours and emotional responses. The beautiful paradox of this is once you get the relationships right they become so quiet, they are almost imperceptible; all the focus is on the work.

## Congruent

Richard Newman (founder of the communication business BodyTalk) emphasises the importance of the congruency of your body language and your words (2018).

Greeting students with a smile goes a long way to making them feel cared for and welcome, but a smile whilst telling them off can do the opposite. It is confusing. Something that you want to avoid being.

This might all sound a little illusive, so I will tie it to an example of what a mindful teacher may or may not do in the classroom. If a child uses bad language in the classroom, stop immediately, and let a look of shock and displeasure register on your face. It is important that they know this matters to you, but do not lose it. Reiterate the schools expectations, then take appropriate action in line with the behaviour policy. In your conversations with the child, keep your focus on the behaviour, never the child. You show you care about how they behave because you care about them, what Dix calls deliberate botheredess (2017). As a result of this, you show that it affects you when they slip up, but it does not shake your whole world. Your students should want to do the right thing in your class but should never feel burdened with your feelings or fear your anger if they transgress.

## Slowing Responses Down

It can be hard to hold yourself when things go wrong in the classroom. Drawing from mindfulness can help. If we slow things down and ensure we are really present – feeling one's feet on the ground can help – we will be more contained and able to model appropriate responses for the students.

My tip is to buy yourself some time. Take a deep breath. Then when you do speak, go quieter and use less words. Keep body language neutral, and use non-verbal communication deliberately for impact. This signals that you are calm, in control and responsive.

## Body Language

Convey self-control through limited and decisive movements. Not only will this make you seem relaxed, but this slowing down will also instill calm in your nervous system even when you do not feel it. The actor's principle of not moving without a purpose can be helpful here too. Use movement to convey a message (for example, use a hand gesture for emphasis) but avoid pacing and fidgeting. Whilst they can have a soothing function for us, they are nothing but a distraction to those listening.

We can apply these insights about body language and posture to our students. Teach them to sit up straight, face forward and have their feet on the floor, not because it looks nice but because it will make them feel calmer, more energised and more focused.

## Breath

Our breath is another useful tool both for keeping ourselves calm and communicating this calm to others. 'Extend the duration of your phrases. Add more words to your phrases before you take a breath', suggests Dr Stephen Porges (2017). This has a calming effect on the heart but also influences our social communication. Porges explains, 'As the vagal regulation of the heart increases, so does the vagal influence on the larynx and pharynx. The voice becomes more melodic and conveys cues to others of safety' (*ibid* p. 192). As we make ourselves calm, we are also physiologically regulating our students.

Use a measured tone and volume at all times. Vary your tone for corrections so that your message is congruent with your response, but keep your tone warm and the volume quiet. If anything, lower your voice a little. A hushed whisper is incredibly powerful in terms of getting students' attention, and it can allow you to make corrections ('Eyes forward, Joe') in the least invasive way possible.

## The Power of Being Present

Being mindful of our pace, tone, body language, breath and congruency with our words will not only make us appear more in control and present; it will actually make us so. This frees us up to be responsive to students' needs, where learning really happens, and reset and regulate them successfully when things go wrong.

The power of responsive teaching once again indicates that we cannot separate the cognitive from the relational. Our experiences of relationships, including teacher-student ones, are profoundly embodied. Polyvagal theory has demonstrated how we can regulate others with our own emotional state. If we are present, our body language conveys this; if we truly listen, we find that we are clear and able to respond. For example, when we take a moment to stand still and breathe before we give instructions, we hold authority in a way that commands our students.

It can sometimes be hard to be present; there is so much external pressure placed on us as teachers and leaders. I know I spent much of my early part of my career 'up in my head'. I did all the *right* things, put hours into my planning, used the systems consistently, and somehow it still did not land. I was too focused on my own performance, already planning the next activity in my own head. I did not pay enough attention to the content of what students were actually learning or what they were writing in their books.

Now I want to be clear it is *not* all on you; children bring what they do to the classroom. There are many reasons for this, for which you are not responsible. However, I do believe that truly being present in the classroom is the closest thing that we have to a silver bullet. This will always be a practise, not a finished event. The techniques in Section One can support you to come back to your body and be in the present moment with the children in front of you if you disappear into your head for a moment. By keeping up this practice, over time it will becomes habitual and embodied, and you will find yourself far more present.

There is an interesting paradox that comes about as a result of being really present. When you focus your attention on being fully in the room, it allows you to notice the subtle cues that students give off: the student who does not pick up a pen or the duo who start chatting when they are meant to be having a focused paired discussion. This information helps you become more responsive and feeds into your planning. Perhaps you check in with the child who has not started writing and see what they are finding difficult, or you adjust your seating plan to separate the chatty pair. As a result, your classroom becomes calmer and more efficient, further reducing the cognitive load for everyone in the classroom and therefore allowing you even more time to be responsive. It is a reinforcing cycle: when you notice and respond to what is happening, things become easier, and because things are easier you can notice more.

## The Joy of Responsive Teaching

Responsive teaching has the power to deepen the dyadic relationship between teacher and student. It both moves children forward academically and provides the possibility for 'corrective emotional experiences' for those young people in need of them. When you listen to students' answers, read their work and respond you are relating to them. You are showing up and being *their* teacher. You are neither a 'sage on the stage' nor a 'guide by the side' but someone who is in relationship with them and their work, offering knowledge, guidance and encouragement.

Academic success cannot be separated from healthy relationships. Learning improves self-esteem by opening up the world to young people and allowing them to feel as though they have a stake in it, that their education is worth something. As teachers this is deeply satisfying. It is the magic of our work and why so many of us, despite the odds, feel compelled to do it. The joy of responsive teaching is that when we strip back the noise and focus on the students in front of us and our love for our subjects, the children feel heard, seen and held and the joy of teaching can shine through.

## Reflection

The children can benefit from techniques to help them be present in the classroom too. Building time for reflection in your lessons is one way to support student regulation. Whilst the Education Endowerment Foundation studies (2018) indicate that meta-cognition is an important area of learning, much like AfL it is often implemented badly and tokenistically. Like anything, reflection needs scaffolding. Break down and model what reflection looks like in its specific context. Link success to effort and keep it low stakes. This is so students are honest with themselves rather than trying to please you or show off. Keep things predictable, perhaps including some short reflection questions at the end of every lesson, but keep it specific too so it does not lose its meaning.

## Regulation

Some of the reflection questions can be academic (*what have I learnt?*) but we need to scaffold emotional regulation too (*how focused was I in today's lesson?*). It can be helpful to have scripts, to draw on in the moment when a student becomes dysregulated. These can calm you as well as them. The following is my tried and tested approach to calming a dysregulated student. In his book *When the Adults Change Everything Changes*, Paul Dix (2017) also offers a range of detailed scripts to get students back on track.

Like anything it is important to understand the principles and then practice them until they feel more natural. You want to convey you are in charge but in a non-threatening way. Get down to the height that the student is, preferably side on or perpendicular rather than facing them, and use a calm and clear voice.

## Approach to Calming a Dysregulated Student

- First, validate their feelings, starting with a sentence like 'I can see you feel it is unfair' or 'I notice that you are very frustrated'.

- Next, name the problem, appealing to general principles or school rules if needed to keep it from being personal: for example, 'In our class we. . .'.

- Explain you know that they are capable of better, perhaps drawing on a previous success: 'I know you are able to. . .'

- Provide a positive choice: 'Why don't we. . .'

- Provide take-up time, perhaps walking away, telling the student something like 'I'll give you thirty seconds to make a good decision.'

- Follow through on whatever you said you were going to do.

Sometimes students need some more physiological regulation too.

## Simple Breathing Activity for Children (Square Breathing)

- Inhale for five seconds.

- Hold your breath for two seconds.

- Exhale for seven seconds.

- Hold your breath for two seconds.

# Reset

Classroom culture can easily slip. When this happens, it is the time when we most strongly need to hold ourselves. We must breathe through any frustration or humiliation and maintain our warm-strict persona. Whilst shouting or threats might work in the short term, as Palmer notes, ultimately, 'when teachers depend on the coercive powers of law or technique, they have no authority at all' (Palmer, 2017, p. 34).

Paul Bambrick-Santoyo's *Get Better Faster* (2016) has some excellent advice for both planned and, in the moment, resets. The intention is to always undertake the least invasive intervention possible. If you can redirect a distracted student without stopping the class, that is excellent. Non-verbal signals, gestures, that infamous teacher stare and using proximity are all highly effective in getting students back on track in a calm, positive and non-distracting manner.

Sometimes a whole class reset is needed. In the moment that might involve you undertaking elements of strong voice (#56), start with self-interrupt; pull a somewhat indignant face. Then square up and stand still, then pause until you have 100 percent compliance. Once you are satisfied that the class is back on track, give clear instructions as to what to do and then pick up the tone and energy once more (Lemov, 2014, pp. 412–416). Keep it breezy, positive and focused on the learning where possible.

There will be times when this will not be enough, and you may need to do a more planned reset, involving reteaching and practicing routines. There really is no shame in bringing in a colleague to support you with this process. It models collaboration and vulnerability; we all need support with behaviour at times, and it reinforces that there are shared expectations across the school to students.

# Restorative Conversations

It is okay to hold boundaries. You are giving the students a good lesson in the long term. Remember Burman's (2014) 'Hate me now, thank me later'. However, there always needs to be chance to repair too. Long restorative conferences are not feasible in the school day, but if a teacher issues a sanction for very poor behaviour, there has been a relationship breakdown, or where there is a repeated pattern (i.e. not because they didn't have a pen one time), then a restorative conversation outside of the classroom is necessary.

It is helpful to set out the parameters of the restorative conversation with the young person first (for example, saying, 'I'm going to speak, then I will give you an opportunity to do so, then we will work out together how we can fix this'). This allows the young person to feel (in attachment aware parlance) 'held in mind'. They know that they will be heard, and you stay in your adult authority by directing the conversation.

Drawing on Gottman and Declaire's (1997) notion of emotion coaching, naming and validating the young person's feelings is very powerful. This attunement allows them to 'feel felt', an experience which is physiologically calming for the nervous system. Acknowledging feelings is not the same as excusing the behaviours that emerge. For example, you can say, 'I am hearing that you are feeling angry' without justifying lashing out as a response. Keeping focused on the specifics of the behaviours that are the problem rather than individuals and personalities matters, as does modelling good listening, appropriate tone and turn taking.

Though I take issue with much of the restorative approaches training because I find it inconsistent and unrealistic to implement, there is one part of a Restorative Justice 4 Schools approach that I have found incredibly helpful. That is their framework for validating feelings and prompting reflection. These very simple reflection questions are effective in supporting a child to understand, take responsibility for their actions and repair relationships. They are as follows:

## Restorative Questions

- What happened?
- What were you thinking/feeling at the time?
- What needs to happen to put it right?
- What are you doing to do differently next time?

(Restorative Justice 4 Schools, 2020)

These conversations can be hard for us as adults, particularly where a child has been downright unpleasant. However, it is our duty to regulate ourselves so that we can show up as adults. That is why we must take reasonability for our own feelings first rather than just pushing them away. The tools in Section One can support you with this.

## Time

It is important to note that none of these techniques are quick fixes. For them to become second nature for you and your students, they are habits that need to be built and reinforced over time. You might not reap the rewards right away. Relationships take time. However, when lesson after lesson, students see that you are consistently there for them, that you follow through on what you say, and the success that they can achieve as a result of a calm, warm classroom they will thank you for it.

## Summary

- A mindful teacher is aware of the impact that their **mood** has on the classroom culture.

- They are the adult in the room and so provide boundaries which allow students to take responsibility for themselves by teaching clear routines and planning for when things go wrong.

- They **emanate calm**, **kindness, regulation** and **presence** through their tone and body language, which allows students to co-regulate.

- Mindful teachers help bring students back on track through **regulation** techniques, **restorative conversations** and **class resets**.

- Through this process of truly being attentive and listening, not only do we move students forward academically by responding to what they know and do not know, but it has the possibility to build 'corrective emotional experiences' by allowing students to feel heard, seen and held.

# Conclusion

This book has drawn on the strength of great leaders. It has explored how they reflect on and engage with the complex and messy reality of their communities, with both love and knowledge. By making the choice to do just a few things well and never losing sight of the human, these leaders provide an antidote to the frantic and performative direction that our profession often takes.

Exploring the paradoxes at the heart of good leadership, the book has put the emerging field of Interpersonal Neurobiology in conversation with Cognitive Science to provide a practical framework to resource your leadership.

This starts with slowing down and doing less, offering grace and humanity towards ourselves, a form of self-parenting. We are then able to extend this out to our school community and make schools safe bases. Schools do not get to be this way without clear expectations and systems that work and are consistently used. It is up to us as adults to get clear on these things and emotionally 'hold' our children. This requires us to be regulated, to listen and be responsive to those around us. It is in this space that true success, both academic and relational, can happen.

It is never either/or; the relational and the academic are two sides of the same coin. However, Cartesian dualism has atomised our thinking. Beyond debates on Twitter, the pendulum of the educational discourse swings back and forth between binary positions. One of the impacts of this has been that the emotional nature of our work has not been seen as having much to do with improving academic outcomes. As such, the impact of emotions on leaders themselves has been neglected.

Finding a middle way, a path of integration or wholeness, requires us to redress this balance. The relational aspect of learning is ironically well backed up empirically. We know that our early experiences shape us. If we are met with co-regulation and safe connection, then secure attachment is the conduit. However, if met by a nervous system that is in fight-or-flight mode or shut down, we may form anxious or ambivalent attachments, which are then echoed in our subsequent relationships. This is as relevant for us as leaders as it is for our students. What we also know is that this is not fixed because we are constantly looking to the others for

 DOI: 10.4324/9781003198482-15

regulation there are plenty of opportunities for 'corrective emotional experiences', which literally rewire our brains.

This is hopeful but also requires us to take the regulation aspect of our job very seriously. As leaders we must model by example and start by taking care of ourselves. This includes reflecting on our own stress patterns. If we acknowledge the connectedness of our mind and body, practice interception and undertake self-care, we can ensure that we stay healthy in our leadership.

From this place we can build a healthy culture that is clear, trusting and puts learning at the heart of everything. This needs to come from the top, and that is not always easy. We must be consistent, congruent, genuine and sometimes a little vulnerable even when this is not comfortable or fashionable.

Thoughtful leaders take plenty of time to engage with research, listen and reflect. They know they cannot do everything and instead choose how they and their teams use their time and energy, doing a few things well. They prioritise systems and relationships, then focus on the core work of curriculum and teaching. They invest in professional development, focused on highest leverage teaching strategies. They provide plenty of opportunities for modelling, practice and feedback on these and develop subject expertise so teachers can develop and deliver a rich curriculum.

Mindful leaders have the humility to know that their work is never done. Whilst they recognise the importance of story and communicating a clear message, they keep their ears open and have the discernment and openness to change when they need to. They know that listening builds trust and gives you insights you would not otherwise be privy to. It lays the groundwork, allowing you to call on discretionary effort and have difficult conversations when they are needed.

To lead mindfully is to acknowledge the paradoxes at the heart of our work. Schools are full of complexity, and so even as it is our work is to simplify, streamline and narrate key messages, this will never fully be done. We deal in complex systems, people and problems. Let us not lose heart; we can make a real difference. Yet we must also have the humility to recognise that we *alone* will not make all the difference. Nonetheless, if we continue to develop our practice, to work on slowing down, doing a few things well and with intention, then reflecting and streamlining further, we can bring more and more people alongside us. If we can do all this whilst also cutting ourselves a break because we know nothing is ever finished or perfect, then we will have found the essence of leading mindfully.

# References

Ainsworth, M. D., & Bowlby, J. (1991). An ethological approach to personality development. *American Psychologist*, *46*(4), 333–341.

Almond, N. (2020). Curriculum coherence: How best to do it? In C. Sealy (Ed.), *The researchED guide to the curriculum*. Woodbridge: John Catt.

Appleyard, K., Egeland, B., van Dulmen, M. H., & Alan Sroufe, L. (2005). When more is not better: The role of cumulative risk in child behavior outcomes. *Journal of Child Psychology and Psychiatry*, *46*(3), 235–245.

Bambrick-Santoyo, P. (2012). *Leverage leadership: A practical guide to building exceptional schools*. San Francisco: Jossey-Bass.

Bambrick-Santoyo, P. (2016). *Get better faster: A 90-day plan for coaching new teachers*. San Francisco: Jossey-Bass.

Barrett, L. F. (2021). *Seven and a half lessons about the brain*. London: Picador.

Bennett, T. (2020). *Running the room: The teachers guide to behaviour*. Woodbridge: John Catt.

Berger, R. (2012, December 8). *Critique and feedback – the story of austin's butterfly – Ron Berger*. Retrieved from www.youtube.com/watch?v=hqh1MRWZjms

Brown, P. C., Roediger, H. L., & McDaniel, M. A. (2014). *Make it stick: The science of successful learning*. Cambridge: Harvard University Press.

Bryk, A. S., & Schneider, B. (2002). *Trust in schools: A core resource for improvement*. New York: Russell Sage Foundation.

Burgess, S. A. (2009). *Test scores, subjective assessment and stereotyping of ethnic minorities*. Bristol: Centre for Market and Public Organisation University of Bristol.

Burman, R. (2014). *Hate me now, thank me later: How to raise your kid with love and limits*. London: Harper Collins.

Cameron, J. (1992). *The artist's way: A spiritual path to higher creativity*. Los Angeles, CA: Jeremy P. Tarcher, Perigee.

Chiesa, A., & Serretti, A. (2009). Mindfulness-based stress reduction for stress management in healthy people: A review and meta-analysis. *The Journal of Alternative and Complementary Medicine*, *15*, 593–600.

Counsell, C. (2018). *Senior curriculum leadership*. Retrieved from https://thedignityoftheth-ingblog.wordpress.com/

Cuddy, A. (2012, June). *Your body language may shape who you are*. Retrieved from www.ted.com/talks/amy_cuddy_your_body_language_may_shape_who_you_are

Mental Health Commission (2011). *The human cost. An overview of the evidence on economic adversity and mental health and recommendations for action.* Dublin: Mental Health Commission.

Dempsey, N. (2020). True inclusion. In S. Locke (Ed.), *The researchED guide to leadership: An evidence-informed guide* (pp. 63–88). Woodbridge: John Catt.

Diamond, J. (2004). *The irritable male syndrome: Managing the four key causes of depression and aggression.* Emmaus, PA: Rodale.

Dix, P. (2017). *When the adults change, everything changes: Seismic shifts in school behaviour.* Carmathen: Independent Thinking Press.

Doidge, N. (2007). *The brain that changes itself.* New York: Penguin.

Dweck, C. (2012). *Mindset: How you can fulfil your potential.* New York: Ballentine Books.

Education Endowment Foundation. (2018, August 30). *Meta cognition and self-regulation.* Education Endowment Foundation. Retrieved from https://educationendowment foundation.org.uk/pdf/generate/?u=https://educationendowmentfoundation.org.uk/pdf/toolkit/?id=138&t=Teaching%20and%20Learning%20Toolkit&e=138&s=

Education Endowment Foundation (2019). *How can schools support parents' engagement in their children's learning?* London: Education Endowment Foundation.

Evans, M. (2020a). *Leaders with substance: An antidote to leadership genericism in schools.* Woodbridge: John Catt.

Evans, M. (2020b). Surviving and thriving in uncertainty. In S. Locke (Ed.), *The researchED guide to leadership: An evidence-informed guide* (pp. 226–240). Woodbridge: John Catt.

Ferguson, R. F. (2003). Teachers' perceptions and expectations and the Black-White test score gap. *Urban Education, 38*(4), 460–507.

Fletcher-Wood, H. (2018). *Responsive teaching: Cognitive science and formative assessment in practice.* London and New York: Routledge.

Fonagy, P., Leigh, T., Steele, M., Steele, H., Kennedy, R., Mattoon, G., . . . Gerber, A. (1996). The relation of attachment status, psychiatric classification, and response to psychotherapy. *Journal of Consulting and Clinical Psychology, 64*(1), 22–31.

Fonagy, P. L. (2021, February). *Children's mental health essential update – the impact of COVID-19, trauma and uncertainty* (Live Video Webinar). Retrieved from https://rm.coe.int/summary-report-of-the-cdenf-webinar-on-covid-19-and-children-s-mental-/1680a4be43

George, C., Kaplan, N., & Main, M. (1985). *The adult attachment interview.* Berkeley: Univeristy of California, Unpublished.

Gilliam, W. S., Maupin, A. N., Reyes, C. R., Accavitti, M., & Shic, F. (2016). *Do early educators' implicit biases regarding sex and race relate to behavior expectations and recommendations of preschool expulsions and suspensions?* New Haven, CT: Yale University Child Study Center.

Gottman, J. M., & Declaire, J. (1997). *Raising an emotionally intelligent child: The heart of parenting.* New York: Fireside.

Gove, M. (2016, June 3). *Sky news: Britons 'have had enough of experts'.* Retrieved from www.youtube.com/watch?v=GGgiGtJk7MA&t=62s

Hamilton, I., Kennard, H., McGushin, A., Höglund-Isaksson, L., Kiesewetter, G., Lott, M., . . . Watts, N. (2021). The public health implications of the Paris agreement: A modelling study. *The Lancet Planetary Health, 5,* e74–e83.

Hawkins, K. (2017). *Mindful teacher, mindful school: Improving wellbeing in teaching and learning.* London: Sage Publications.

Haye, M. (2016, April 8). What isn't working in the transfer from statement to EHCP. *Special Needs Jungle*. Retrieved from www.specialneedsjungle.com/what-isnt-working-in-the-transfer-from-statement-to-ehcp/

Hochschild, A. R. (1983). *The managed heart: The commercialization of human feeling*. Berkeley, CA: University of California Press.

Howard, K. (2020). *Stop talking about wellbeing*. Woodbridge: John Catt.

Hutchinson, J. (2020). Professional development through instructional coaching. In S. Locke (Ed.), *The researchED guide to leadership: An evidence-informed guide* (pp. 211–225). Woodbridge: John Catt.

Isaksen, B. (2015). Bikes. *Red or Green Pen*. Retrieved from https://redorgreenpen.wordpress.com/2015/07/11/bikes/

Kabat-Zinn, J. (2003). Mindfulness-based interventions in context: Past, present, and future. *Clinical Psychology: Science and Practice, 10*, 144–156.

Khoury, B., Lecomte, T., Fortin, G., Masse, M., Therien, P., Bouchard, V., . . . Hofmann, S. (2013). Mindfulness-based therapy: A comprehensive meta-analysis. *Clinical Psychology Review, 33*(6), 763–771.

Kirschner, P., Sweller, J., & Clark, R. E. (2006). Why minimal guidance during instruction does not work: An analysis of the failure of constructivist, discovery, problem-based, experiential, and inquiry-based teaching. *Educational Psychologist, 41*, 75–86.

Knight, O. (2018). *Hate me now thank me later*. Retrieved from https://disciplinarythinking.com/2018/09/17/hate-me-now-thank-me-later/

Kobak, R. R., & Hazan, C. (1991). Attachment in marriage: Effects of security and accuracy of working models. *Journal of Personality and Social Psychology, 60*(6), 861–869.

Konturek, P. C., Brzozowski, T., & Konturek, S. J. (2011, December). Stress and the gut: Pathophysiology, clinical consequences, diagnostic approach and treatment options. *Journal of Physiology and Pharmacology, 62*(6), 591–599.

Lane, S. (2020). *Beyond wiping noses: Building an informed approach to pastoral leadership in schools*. Staffordshire: Crown House Publishing.

Lawrence, N. (2020). *Supervision in education – healthier schools for all*. Barnardo's Scotland report on the use of Professional or Reflective Supervision in Education. Retrieved from https://www.barnardos.org.uk/sites/default/files/uploads/Supervision%20in%20Education%20-%20Healthier%20Schools%20For%20All%20-%20Main%20report_0.pdf

Lemov, D. (2014). *Teach like a champion 2.0: 62 techniques that put students on the path to college*. San Francisco: Jossey-Bass.

Lemov, D. (2016). *Reading reconsidered: A practical guide to rigorous literacy instruction*. San Francisco: Jossey-Bass.

Lorde, A. (1984). The master's tools will never dismantle the master's house. In A. Lorde (Ed.), in *Sister outsider* (pp. 110–113). New York: Sister Visions Press.

Lovell, O. (2020). *Sweller's cognitive load theory in action*. Woodbridge: John Catt.

Marmott, M. (2010). *Fair society healthy lives: Strategic review of health inequalities in England*. London: The Marmott Review.

Mate, G. (2003). *When the body says no: The cost of hidden stress*. London: Penguin, Random House.

May, K. (2020). *Wintering: The power of rest and retreat in difficult times*. London: Rider, Penguin, Random House.

Mccrea, P. (2017). *Memorable teaching: Leveraging memory to build deep and durable learning in the classroom.* Scotts Valley, CA: CreateSpace Independent Publishing Platform.

McCrory, E. (2020). The case for a preventative approach to mental health: Childhood maltreatment, neuroimaging, and the theory of latent vulnerability. In W. Davies, J. Savulescu, & R. Roache (Eds.), *Psychiatry reborn: Biopsychosocial psychiatry in modern medicine.* Oxford: Oxford University Press.

Munby, S. (2020). *A new paradigm for leadership development?* Melbourne: Centre for Strategic Education.

Myatt, M. (2007). *Walking the talk.* Retrieved from www.matrymyatt.com/blog/2017-12-09/walking-the-talk

Myatt, M. (2016). *High challenge, low threat: How the best leaders find the balance.* Woodbridge: John Catt.

Myatt, M. (2020). *Back on track: Fewer things, greater depth.* Woodridge: John Catt.

NASUWT. (2021, May 20). *Violence and abuse of teachers at risk of becoming normalised in Scottish schools.* Retrieved from www.nasuwt.org.uk/article-listing/violence-abuse-teachers-risk-becoming-normalised.html

Neville, B. (2013). Emotion and school: Understanding how the hidden curriculum influences relationships, leadership, teaching, and learning, advances. *Research on Teaching, 18,* 3–23.

Newman, R. (2018). *You were born to speak.* Retrieved from https://www.biblio.com/book/you-were-born-speak-richard-newman/d/1254224877

Newmark, B. (2021, May 4). *How I start a lesson.* Retrieved from https://bennewmark.wordpress.com/2021/05/04/how-i-start-a-lesson/

OECD. (2019). *TALIS 2018 results (Volume I): Teachers and school leaders as lifelong learners.* Paris: TALIS, OECD Publishing.

Ofsted. (2019a). *Inspecting safeguarding in early years, education and skills.* Retrieved from www.gov.uk

Ofsted. (2019b, July 22). *Summary and recommendations: Teacher well-being research report.* Retrieved from www.gov.uk/government/publications/teacher-well-being-at-work-in-schools-and-further-education-providers/summary-and-recommendations-teacher-well-being-research-report

Ofsted. (2021). *Research and analysis: Review of sexual abuse in schools and colleges.* Retrieved from https://www.gov.uk/government/publications/review-of-sexual-abuse-in-schools-and-colleges/review-of-sexual-abuse-in-schools-and-colleges#conclusion

Palmer, P. J. (2017). *The courage to teach: Exploring the inner landscape of a teacher's life.* New York: Wiley.

Pinkett, M., & Roberts, M. (2019). *Boys don't try? Rethinking masculinity in schools.* New York and London: Routledge.

Popper, M., & Mayseless, O. (2003). Back to basics: Applying a parenting perspective to transformational leadership. *The Leadership Quaterly, 14*(1), 41–65.

Porges, S. W. (2017). *The pocket guide to the polyvagal theory: The transformative power of feeling safe.* Norton Series on Interpersonal Neurobiology. New York and London: W. W. Norton & Company.

Ramlakhan, N. (2010). *Tired but wired: How to overcome sleep problems: The essential sleep toolkit.* London: Souvenir Press Ltd.

Reid, A. (2018, October 30). *Parents and teachers for excellence*. Retrieved from https://parentsandteachers.org.uk/curriculum-critical-theory-and-conversation-why-the-right-dont-need-to-dominate-the-discussion/

Reid, A. (2020, August 6). *Structural racism or unconscious bias: That time a parent called me racist*. Retrieved from https://streamlinedsendco.com/2020/08/06/structural-racism-or-unconscious-bias-that-time-a-parent-called-me-racist/

Restorative Justice 4 Schools. (2020). *Restorative justice for schools*. Retrieved from www.restorativejustice4schools.co.uk/wp/?page_id=26

Riley, P. (2011). *Attachment theory and the teacher–student relationship: A practical guide for teachers, teacher educators and school leaders*. London and New York: Routledge.

Rizzolatti, G., & Craighero, L. (2004). The mirror-neuron system. *Annual Review of Neuroscience, 27*(1), 169–192.

Robinson, V. (2011). *Student-centred leadership*. San Francisco: Jossey-Bass.

Roeser, R. W., Skinner, E., Beers, J., & Jennings, P. A. (2012). Mindfulness training and teachers' professional development: An emerging area of research and practice. *Child Development Perspectives, 6*, 167–173.

Rosenshine, B. (2012, Spring). Principles of instruction: Research-based strategies that all teachers should know. *American Educator*, 12–39.

Scharfe, E., & Bartholomew, K. (1994). Reliability and stability of adult attachment patterns. *Personal Relationships, 1*, 23–43.

Sedlmeier, P., Eberth, J., Schwarz, M., Zimmermann, D., Haarig, F., Jaeger, S., & Kunze, S. (2012, November). The psychological effects of meditation: A meta-analysis. *Psychological Bulletin, 138*(6), 1139–1171.

Sergiovanni, T. J. (2005). *Strengthening the heartbeat: Leading and learning together in schools*. San Francisco, CA: Jossey-Bass.

Sherrington, T. (2019). *Rosenshine's principles in action*. Woodbridge: John Catt.

Short, C. (2021, June 8). *Wellbeing talk* (C. Short, Performer). Bristol: Bristol Grammar School.

Siegal, D. J. (2012). *The pocket guide to interpersonal neurobiology: An integrative handbook for the mind*. New York and London: W. W. Norton & Company.

Spielman, A. (2017, October). Retrieved from www.gov.uk/government/speeches/hmcis-commentary-october-2017

Stanovich, K. (1986). Matthew effects in reading: Some consequences of individual differences in the acquisition of literacy. *Reading Research Quarterly, 21*, 360–407.

Thom, J. (2018). *Slow teaching: On finding calm, clarity and impact in the classroom*. Woodbridge: John Catt.

Tomsett, J. (n.d.). Retrieved from www.johntomsett.com/

Van der Kolk, B. (2015). *The body keeps the score: Brain, mind, and body in the healing of trauma*. New York: Penguin Random House.

Waterman, C. (2020, May 12). *Love and knowledge in leadership—talk*. Retrieved from https://researched.org.uk/2020/05/12/carly-waterman-love-and-knowledge-in-leadership/

Webster, R. (2021, May 18). *Why Ofsted is wrong about TA support for SEND pupils*. Retrieved from www.tes.com/news/teaching-assistants-why-ofsted-has-no-idea-how-use-tas-support-send

Webster, R., & Blatchford, P. (2013). The educational experiences of pupils with a statement for special educational needs in mainstream primary schools: Results from a systematic observation study. *European Journal of Special Needs Education, 28*(4), 463.

Webster, R., & Blatchford, P. (2019). Making sense of 'teaching', 'support' and 'differentiation': The educational experiences of pupils with education, health and care plans and statements in mainstream secondary schools. *European Journal of Special Needs, 34*(1), 98–113.

Whitworth, D. (2019, February 23). Higher education: The inner-city teacher who took his students up a mountain. *The Sunday Times*. Retrieved from www.thetimes.co.uk/article/higher-education-the-inner-city-teacher-who-took-his-students-up-a-mountain-g9gcn5kzv

Willingham, D. T. (2008–2009, Winter). Ask the cognitive scientist. *American Educator*, 17–44.

Winnicott, D. W. (2002). *Winnicott on the child*. Cambridge, MA: Perseus Publishing.

Worth, J. (2018). *National foundation for educational research*. Retrieved from www.nfer.ac.uk/news-events/nfer-blogs/latest-teacher-retention-statistics-paint-a-bleak-picture-for-teacher-supply-in-england/

Young, M. (2014). *Knowledge and the future school: Curriculum and social justice*. London: Bloomsbury.

Young, M. (2018). A knowledge-led curriculum: Pitfalls and possibilities. *Impact; Journal of the Chartered College of Teaching*, 1–4.

Zamperoni, V. (2017). *Mental health foundation*. Retrieved from www.mentalhealth.org.uk/blog/what-new-statistics-show-about-childrens-mental-health

# Index

Note: Page numbers in *italics* indicate a figure on the corresponding page.

Ingram Content Group UK Ltd.
Milton Keynes UK
UKHW021459170323
418657UK00020B/282

9 781032 056364